MUSIC AND THE MASS

A Practical Guide for Ministers of Music

THE MASS

A Practical Guide for Ministers of Music

DAVID HAAS

LITURGY
TRAINING
PUBLICATIONS

Acknowledgments

All quotations from scripture, except as noted below, are taken from the *New Revised Standard Version* of the Bible, copyright © 1989, Division of Christian Education of the National Council of the Churches of Christ of the United States of America. Published by Oxford University Press, Inc., New York. Used with permission. All rights reserved.

Psalm 104:30 is from the *Contemporary English Version* (CEV) of the Bible, © 1991, American Bible Society. All rights reserved. Used with permission.

The English translation of the lenten gospel acclamation from the *Lectionary for Mass* © 1969, International Committee on English in the Liturgy, Inc. (ICEL); the English translation of the *Attende, Domine* from *Resource Collection of Hymns and Service Music for the Liturgy* © 1981, ICEL; excerpts from the English translation of the *Constitution on the Sacred Liturgy, The General Instruction of the Roman Missal,* and the *Directory for Masses with Children* from *Documents on the Liturgy, 1963 – 1979: Conciliar, Papal and Curial Texts* © 1982, ICEL; the English translation of the psalms and of Judith 16, Wisdom 16:20 – 21, Sirach 14:20, 15:3, Ezekiel 36:24 – 25, 1 Timothy 3:16 and Revelation 19:6 from the *Liturgical Psalter* © 1994, ICEL; excerpts from the English translation of the Introduction to the *Lectionary for Mass* (Second Typical Edition) © 1981, ICEL and altered by the National Conference of Catholic Bishops in 1998. All rights reserved.

Excerpts from the *Appendix to the General Instruction of the Roman Missal for the Dioceses of the United States* © 1982, United States Catholic Conference (USCC), Washington DC; *Music in Catholic Worship* © 1983, USCC; *Liturgical Music Today* © 1982, USCC; *Environment and Art in Catholic Worship* © 1978, USCC; *Fulfilled in Your Hearing* © 1982, USCC; *Plenty Good Room* © 1990, USCC; and *The Place of Music in the Eucharistic Celebration,* © 1967, USCC, are used by license of the copyright owner. All rights reserved.

This book was edited by Victoria M. Tufano. Audrey Novak Riley was the production editor. The book was designed by Jill Smith, and Phyllis Martinez was the production artist. The typefaces used in this book are Veljovic and Charme. It was printed by Bawden Printing, Eldridge, Iowa.

Library of Congress Catalog Card Number: 98-87476

ISBN 1-56854-198-8

MUSMAS

Contents

Introduction

Much has been written about the ministry of music in Roman Catholic worship since the Second Vatican Council. Some of these many books and articles have acclaimed the development and creativity of recent years; others have criticized the level of quality of the repertoire or the professionalism of those who lead music in our parish communities.

The repertoire now available to parish musicians consists of an endless library of hymns, psalms, songs and acclamations. There are many opportunities for parish musicians to grow in their ministry through the many workshops, seminars and conventions of liturgists and musicians held annually throughout North America. These and other resources have contributed greatly to the skills of those charged with the ministry of sung prayer, and in a growing desire among musicians for more knowledge about our central activity as believers, that is, about our gathering on Sunday to feast upon God's word and meal.

Many of us who serve as pastoral musicians were trained in the arts of music and musical performance, not in the skills of liturgical celebration and ministerial leadership. There is a great thirst among music ministers to become liturgically literate. However, most don't have the time or resources to go back to school for a degree in liturgical studies. For many who lead music on Sunday, mentors and teachers who can hand on the necessary knowledge and skills are difficult to find. Many music ministers are volunteers with other jobs and other commitments that must take precedence. For them, and for many full-time professional liturgical musicians, the project of studying the vast field of church history and the church's many official documents on the liturgy alongside their regular responsibilities is simply too much. Yet all of us involved in music ministry need to continue to grow in knowledge and skills; we are never finished learning our ministry.

About This Book

To help with this continuing task, I have compiled this book. It is a basic guidebook whose goal is to point musicians and liturgical ministers toward key documents and principles of the celebration of the eucharist. This is a "walk-through" of the Mass, rite by rite and step by step. Each chapter in this book considers one of the main divisions of the Mass and the elements of that division. These main divisions are the introductory rites, the liturgy of the word, the liturgy of the eucharist (including the preparatory rites) and the closing rites. Each element within these divisions is discussed, with original commentary and pertinent excerpts from scripture, church documents and various other sources.

Scripture

Our ritual prayer has its origins in the Hebrew and Christian scriptures. As liturgical ministers, we need to appreciate the biblical roots of our liturgy and our ministry. In the scriptures we find not only the roots of our ritual acts and texts, but also the sources of our spirituality and theology of the rites. The discussions of each liturgical action in this book include quotations from the biblical sources that are at the root of that liturgical action, or passages that can illuminate our understanding of that action.

Documentation

Many music ministers have been trained as musicians, not as liturgists. We need to become familiar with the documents and principles that direct our celebrations. It is not possible to include the full texts of all the relevant church documents in a book of this scope, but musicians will find excerpts necessary to understand various liturgical moments and elements. The documents most quoted and referred to here are these:

The Constitution on the Sacred Liturgy
This is the source document, the mandate given by the church at the Second Vatican Council for the reform of the liturgy (1963).

The General Instruction of the Roman Missal
This is the introduction and "owner's manual" for the sacramentary, the book that contains the presider's prayers and rubrics (directions) for the Mass. The General Instruction offers a step-by-step examination of the Mass along with such other essential information as guidelines for church furnishings, vessels and vestments (1969).

Appendix to the General Instruction for the Dioceses of the United States
The bishops of the United States offer additional instruction for the celebration of Mass in the United States (1974).

Lectionary for Mass: Introduction
This document offers an excellent introduction to the use of scripture in Catholic liturgy. It also presents the plan and order of the lectionary, the book of scripture readings for the Mass (revised edition, 1981).

Directory for Masses with Children
This document, written to provide guidance for the celebration of Mass when children are present in the assembly, is also useful for preparing Mass with adults (1973).

Music in Catholic Worship
The United States' Bishops' Committee on the Liturgy (BCL) published this guideline for the pastoral use of music in the liturgy (1972).

Liturgical Music Today
This sequel and companion to *Music in Catholic Worship* addresses issues raised in the ten years between the publication of the two documents (1982).

Environment and Art in Catholic Worship
This BCL document offers guidance on architecture, furnishings, vessels, vesture and images in Catholic churches (1978).

Fulfilled in Your Hearing
The U.S. Bishops' Committee on Priestly Life and Ministry published this document, which not only explores the role of the homily and the preacher in the liturgy, but also offers a method for preparing the homily (1982).

Plenty Good Room
This document, subtitled "The Spirit and Truth of African American Catholic Worship," was written by the U.S. Bishops' Committees on Liturgy and on Black Catholics. It encourages the adaptation of the liturgy to the style and culture of the African American community, and offers guidelines for inculturation that can be used by many cultural groups (1990).

Pastoral musicians will benefit from reading these documents and keeping copies for reference. All of them are available individually. Liturgy Training Publications' *The Liturgy Documents* (available as a book and on disk) contains all these documents except *Plenty Good Room,* which is available from the United States Catholic Conference and from LTP.

Other Sources

In addition to scripture passages and excerpts from the liturgical documents, you will find quotations from other sources. There are excerpts from early church documents, texts of hymns and songs that articulate a vision of the ritual action under discussion and "quotable quotes" from contemporary liturgical scholars and heroes that may be helpful in getting inside the meaning of the rites.

Background and Commentary

The section on each liturgical element concludes with a brief and basic history of that part of the Mass and commentary on present pastoral practice. The commentary also offers ideas and options for moments of the Mass that affect the rite under discussion, which may influence choices and decisions about music. Because I am a music minister and practitioner, not a professional liturgist, my comments are aimed mostly at issues that affect music and the ministry of music. I will leave it to others to dig into the more advanced liturgical issues.

Using This Book

It is useful to have at hand a copy of the lectionary and the sacramentary when using this resource. These two ritual books are foundational to all of the elements, issues and topics raised here, and are central to any discussion or study of the Mass.

This book is not intended to present an answer for every question that might arise for a music minister about the eucharistic celebration, nor is it meant to serve as an inexhaustible well of ideas for musical creativity in liturgy. However, I hope it can provide musicians and other liturgical ministers with some information that is essential to this ministry, and serve as a springboard to greater creativity and knowledge. To encourage that, this book provides room for your ideas and thoughts. This book could also serve as a workbook for continuing education for parish music ministers, as a journal for preserving good ideas and as a source of inspiration.

Thank You

Any knowledge, skills or insights have come to me from wonderful teachers, mentors and friends who have shared their genius, scholarship and practical wisdom. I remember especially the late and beloved friends and mentors Eugene Walsh, Ralph Keifer, Sue Martin and James Dunning, of whom I have wonderful memories of sharing meals, workshops and conversations, and from whom I learned more than any textbook could offer.

I also want to thank friends, teachers and heroes who have shaped my own love and knowledge of the liturgy: Richard Fragomeni, Vicky Tufano, Ed Foley, Don Neumann, Bob Duggan, Paul Covino, John Wright, Ron Lewinski, Bishop Kenneth Untener, Lizette Larson-Miller, Ray East, James Moudry, George DeCosta, James Bessert, Don Saliers and Archbishop Rembert Weakland. I am also grateful to my fellow composers and colleagues in music ministry, who inspire me by their tireless commitment to quality ministry and music in liturgy: Marty Haugen, Bob Batastini, Christopher Walker, Rob Glover, Lori True, Leon Roberts, Stephen Petrunak, Mary Werner, Frank Brownstead, Rob Strusinski, Bob Hurd, Kate Cuddy, Fran O'Brien, Fred Moleck, Joe Camacho, Bonnie Faber, Rory Cooney, Dan Schutte, Carol Porter, David Anderson, Mary Beth Kunde-Anderson, Jo Infante, Mike Hay, Derek Campbell and Gary Daigle. Thanks also to my friend Arthur Zannoni, who has helped me to delve into and understand the riches of the scriptures. And finally, I want to express my deepest thanks and gratitude to Michael Joncas, who has been teacher, mentor, friend and witness in my ministry, and whose love and tireless study of the liturgy is truly a gift to a worshiping church that needs always to travel the road of renewal. It is to him that this resource is dedicated.

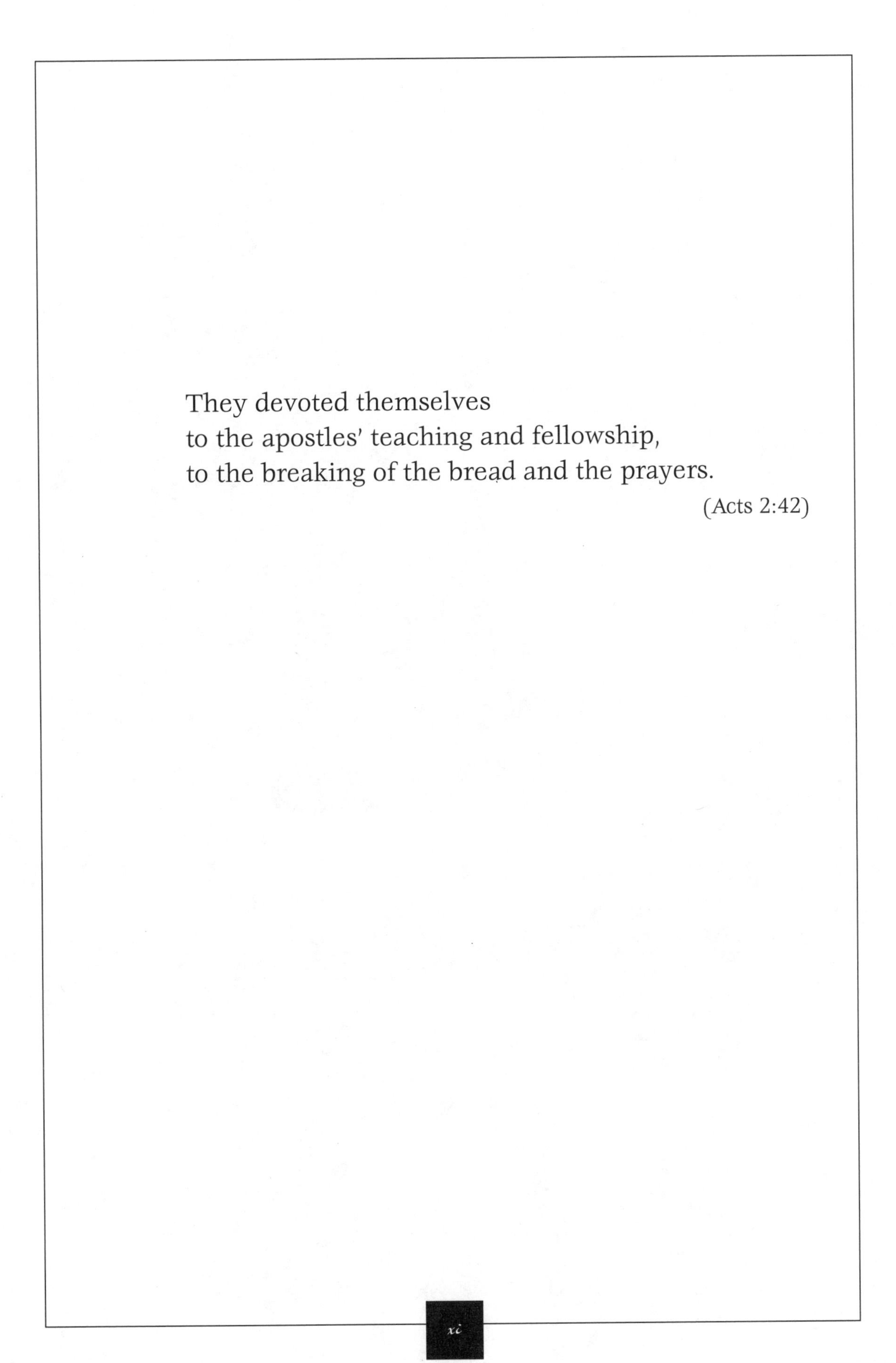

They devoted themselves
to the apostles' teaching and fellowship,
to the breaking of the bread and the prayers.

(Acts 2:42)

chapter ONE

The Gathering Rites

General Background

Scripture

Lord, who is welcome in your house?
Who can rest on your holy mountain?
Those who walk with integrity
and do only what is right,
speaking the truth with courage.

Psalm 15:1–2

When the day of Pentecost had come, they were all together in one place.

Acts 2:1

For where two or three are gathered in my name, I am there among them.

Matthew 18:20

Documentation

For on this day Christ's faithful must gather together so that, by hearing the word of God and taking part in the eucharist, they may call to mind the passion, the resurrection, and the glorification of the Lord Jesus and may thank God, who "has begotten them again unto a living hope through the resurrection of Jesus Christ from the dead" (1 Peter 1:3).

Constitution on the Sacred Liturgy, 106

The purpose of these rites is that the faithful coming together take on the form of a community.

General Instruction of the Roman Missal, 24

A fully Christian life is inconceivable without participation in the liturgical services in which the faithful, gathered into a single assembly, celebrate the paschal mystery.

Directory for Masses with Children, 8

The purpose of these rites is to help the assembled people become a worshiping community and to prepare them for listening to God's Word and celebrating the Eucharist (GIRM, 24). Of these parts the entrance song and the opening prayer are primary. All else is secondary.

Music in Catholic Worship, 44

The church, therefore, is first and foremost a gathering of those whom the Lord has called into a covenant of peace with himself. In this gathering, as in every other, offices and ministries are necessary, but secondary. The primary reality is Christ in the assembly, the People of God.

Fulfilled in Your Hearing, 5

The Eucharistic assembly that gathers Sunday after Sunday is a rich and complex phenomenon. Even in parishes that are more or less uniform in ethnic, social, or economic background, there is great diversity: men and women, old and young, the successes and the failures, the joyful and the bereaved, the fervent and the halfhearted, the strong and the weak. Such diversity is a constant challenge.

Fulfilled in Your Hearing, 8

The assembly gathers for liturgy as a community of faith, believing that God has acted in human history and more particularly, in their own history.

Fulfilled in Your Hearing, 12

Gathering for liturgy is a time of glory and praise. Gathering for liturgy is "passing time" with the Lord. It is time to heal the "sin-sick" soul. It is a time to give the Spirit breathing room. It is time to tell the ancient story, at dawn and at dusk, on Sunday, and in every season.

Plenty Good Room, 91

In a liturgical celebration, the whole assembly is *leitourgos,* each member according to his own function. The baptismal priesthood is that of the whole Body of Christ.

The Catechism of the Catholic Church, 1188

Other Sources

On the day named after the sun, all who live in city or countryside assemble. . . . It is on Sunday that we all assemble, because Sunday is the first day: the day on which God transformed darkness and matter and created the world, and the day on which Jesus Christ our Savior rose from the dead.

Justin Martyr

It is the people, God's holy people, that make up the church, that *need* the liturgy. For the liturgy is not created nor made up by the church. It is received from God, but it can only exist for the people.

Paul Hallinan

The mission of Christ, the mission of the church, the liturgy of the church, all demand contact of the faithful with the living channels of Christ's action here on earth. Without participation of the faithful in the liturgy, these channels have no meaning, no efficacy.

Virgil Michel

Gathering is the energy that has the power to transform a passive people into a consciously active people. It is precisely by means of gathering that members of the assembly begin transforming themselves from passive receivers to active doers.

Eugene Walsh

Background and Commentary

The opening rites as we find them in the present structure (song, greeting, sign of the cross, sprinkling rite or penitential rite, Kyrie, Gloria, opening prayer) were gradual additions to the liturgy, which originally began simply, with the proclamation of the scriptures. The initial rites varied by region, and by the early Middle Ages they included a wide variety of prayers. The purpose of these gathering or introductory rites are twofold: to help the community gather and form itself, and to prepare the community to listen attentively to the word of God. The elements of the time of gathering that will be discussed in this chapter are:

Entering, Gathering and Hospitality
Preparation Time
Song of Gathering
Sign of the Cross and Greeting
Rite of Blessing and Sprinkling of Holy Water
Penitential Rite or Kyrie
Gloria
Opening Prayer

These rites are not unified, but inconsistent in their content and intent. They can be confusing to understand and difficult to plan. Often, in practice, they are simply too long. The opening rites of the liturgy, which are intended to serve as a focused preparation to encounter God's word, often become cumbersome and top-heavy. Those who prepare the liturgy should remember that the key elements of the introductory rites are the opening song and the opening prayer.

The primary focus of these beginning rites is the gathered assembly; they should be the primary consideration in the planning and preparation (just as they must be throughout the celebration). If the primacy of the assembly is lost or buried in these rites, those who prepare the liturgy must re-evaluate how these rites are celebrated and experienced.

Entering, Gathering and Hospitality

Scripture

I am sure God is here,
right beside me.

Psalm 16:8a

Whoever welcomes you welcomes me, and whoever welcomes me welcomes the one who sent me.

Matthew 10:40

Greet one another with a holy kiss.

1 Corinthians 16:20

I appeal to you therefore, brothers and sisters, by the mercies of God, to present your bodies as a living sacrifice, holy and acceptable to God, which is your spiritual worship.

Romans 12:1

There is no longer Jew or Greek, there is no longer slave or free, there is no longer male and female; for all of you are one in Christ Jesus.

Galatians 3:28

So then you are no longer strangers and aliens, but you are citizens with the saints and also members of the household of God, built upon the foundation of the apostles and prophets, with Christ Jesus himself as the cornerstone. In him the whole structure is joined together and grows into a holy temple in the Lord; in whom you also are built together spiritually into a dwelling place for God.

Ephesians 2:19 – 22

Documentation

The Church, therefore, earnestly desires that Christ's faithful, when present at this mystery of faith, should not be there as strangers or silent spectators.

Constitution on the Sacred Liturgy, 48

In the celebration of Mass the faithful are a holy people, a people God has made his own, a royal priesthood: . . . They should endeavor to make this clear by their deep sense of reverence for God and their charity toward all who share with them in the celebration. They therefore are to shun any appearance of individualism or division, keeping before their mind that they have the one Father in heaven and therefore are all brothers and sisters to each other. They should become one body.

General Instruction of the Roman Missal, 62

As common prayer and ecclesial experience, liturgy flourishes in a climate of hospitality: a situation in which people are comfortable with one another, either knowing or being introduced to one another; a space in which people are seated together, with mobility, in view of one another as well as the focal points of the rite, involved as participants and *not* as spectators (GIRM, 4, 5).

Environment and Art in Catholic Worship, 11

Among the symbols with which liturgy deals, none is more important than this assembly of believers.

Environment and Art in Catholic Worship, 28

Worship is always a celebration of community. Because in this spirituality, "I" takes its meaning from "we."

Plenty Good Room, 84

Other Sources

Come together on the Lord's day,
break bread and give thanks,
having first confessed your sins
so that your sacrifice may be pure.
Anyone who has a quarrel with his fellow
should not gather with you
until he has been reconciled,
lest your sacrifice be profaned.

Didache

Command and exhort the people to be faithful to the assembly of the church. Let them not fail to attend, but let them gather faithfully together. Let no one deprive the church by staying away; if they do, they deprive the body of Christ of one of its members!

Didascalia of the Apostles

Liturgy is the way Christians behave in the presence of the living God.

Aidan Kavanagh

When the members of the assembly take personal responsibility for gathering and being hospitable at Sunday Mass, you begin to have genuine, active participation.

Eugene Walsh

Create a climate where no one is stranger, where families become family, where even the enemy is loved.

Thomas Banick

When the people are open to the holy in themselves, they will more readily recognize it elsewhere.

Karen Clarke

Think assembly! Focus assembly! Get a single-minded preoccupation with one only question: How can we help the assembly bring itself to life?

Eugene Walsh

Coming to church is coming home. . . . When the assembly gathers, people gather to have their deepest hungers nourished and to nourish the hungers of others.

John Gallen

To offer hospitality to a stranger is to welcome something new, unfamilia, and unknown in our life-world. On the one hand, hospitality requires recognition of the stranger's vulnerability in an alien social world. Strangers need shelter and sustenance in their travels, especially when they are moving through a hostile environment. On the other hand, hospitality designates occasions of potential discovery which can open up our narrow, provincial worlds. Strangers have stories to tell which we have never heard before, stories which can redirect our seeing and stimulate our imaginations. The stories invite us to view the world from a novel perspective. They display the finitude and relativity of our own orientation to meaning. The sharing of stories may prove threatening, but not necessarily so. It may generate a festive mood, a joy in celebrating the meeting of minds across social and cultural differences. The stranger does not simply challenge or subvert our assumed world of meaning; she may enrich, even transform the world.

Thomas Ogletree

Hospitality is the embrace that a person or community extends to others, gathering them into the life of one's own.

John Gallen

Background and Commentary

Hospitality is essential to worship. It is fascinating to note that *Environment and Art in Catholic Worship* is concerned first with the hospitality of the environment, before it begins to address furnishings and decorations:

> Liturgy flourishes in a climate of hospitality: a situation in which people are comfortable with one another, either knowing or being introduced to one another; a space in which people are seated together, with mobility, in view of one another as well as the focal points of the rite, involved as participants and not as spectators. (11)

Music ministers share with all the liturgical ministers, including the assembly, responsibility to create the atmosphere of hospitality that is so important to a life-giving liturgical experience. Our role in creating this climate is not fulfilled by how well we sing, but by our deportment and behavior when we are not singing. Often, we are the first people whom the assembly encounters (with the exception, we hope, of the ministers of hospitality) in a public manner. The way in which we conduct ourselves before the liturgy begins is a vital aspect of our ministry; it affects our ability to lead and minister throughout the liturgical experience. Are we accessible before the liturgy begins? Are we out in the body of the worship space greeting and welcoming people, or are we hiding in the sacristy with each other, and then coming out at the last minute to announce the opening song? Are we ready and rehearsed well before the liturgy begins, or are we practicing, tuning our instruments and talking among ourselves in front of the assembly ten minutes before the liturgy begins? Through these behaviors we influence how the assembly feels about their place in the liturgical experience. Even before the liturgy begins and before a note of music is played, we can nourish (or not) their sense of ownership and participation.

All of us music ministers should set this simple goal for ourselves: to have everything prepared and ready to go at least fifteen minutes before the liturgy begins. This includes having the music in order, the instruments tuned, the vocal warm-ups completed, the microphones set — everything completely ready. This frees the cantor and members of the choir or ensemble to be present in the worship or gathering space and to share in the ministry of welcoming and greeting the assembly. Then, a minute or so before the liturgy begins, they can take their places and assume their leadership role.

My experience (as well as the experience of ministers in many other communities) has been that this establishes a wonderful rapport between the ministers and the assembly, and helps foster a sense of comfort and belonging, resulting in a visible change in the quality of participation over time. A relationship is established, and the assembly grows in their awareness of being fellow worshipers. This is something that no bulletin announcement or adult education class could give.

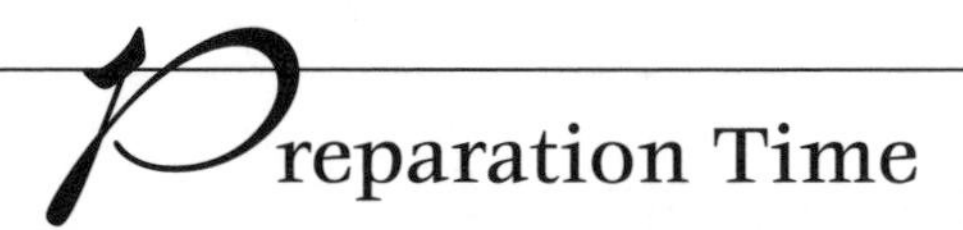

Preparation Time

Scripture

Prepare the way of the Lord.

Mark 1:3

Documentation

Through a good understanding of the rites and prayers they should take part in the sacred service conscious of what they are doing, with devotion and full involvement.

Constitution on the Sacred Liturgy, 48

Other Sources

If you're happy to be here, inform your face.

Eugene Walsh

People will sing things that are familiar.

Frank Brownstead

The preparation should be simple, short and friendly. The musician should greet the people informally and informatively, go over any music that needs to taught or reviewed, and sympathetically encourage the people to sing.

Elaine Rendler

To begin, less is more. It is far better to introduce a few tunes and to learn them well.

Bob Batastini

Background and Commentary

Many choirs or contemporary ensembles provide a prelude or solo selection before the gathering song that officially begins the liturgy. The intention is to provide a prayerful mood for the liturgy. However, inviting the assembly to listen to a musical selection in a receptive and passive attitude can be a problem. Some ethnic communities have traditions of prelude music that involves the assembly, that warms up the community to worship together.

Instrumental preludes may also invite passivity in the assembly. This is not to say that instrumental prelude music is inappropriate. Rather, the musician needs to think through the nature and spirit of the selection. Will the prelude's compositional nature encourage an atmosphere of friendliness and hospitality, or will it cause the members of the assembly to withdraw into themselves, becoming passive or isolated? Instrumental music can provide a wonderful ambiance for people to connect with one another. But choices have to be made carefully. Prelude music should not confuse the assembly about their role in the liturgy.

Having a musical rehearsal with the assembly is important in preparing the assembly to pray together. This rehearsal is more than just teaching the assembly a new piece of music. More importantly, it is an act of hospitality. Taking time to rehearse with the assembly subtly says: "We care about you. We want you to share this experience with us. We believe that you are the body of Christ. Your participation in this prayer of thanks and praise is important."

The liturgy begins when the people leave their cars in the parking lot and enter the worship space. Hospitality, visual and aural environment, rehearsal with the assembly — these intensely important factors in a sense constitute the beginning of the worship experience itself. Everything that follows will depend on these beginning moments.

Song of Gathering

Scripture

Shake tambourines! Clash cymbals!
Strike up a song to my God!
Sound a new music of praise!
Praise and call on God's name!
I sing my God a fresh new song:
"Grandeur and glory are yours, Lord,
with power that astonishes all."

Judith 16:2 – 3, 13a

Stretch toward heaven, you gates,
open high and wide.
Let the glorious sovereign enter.

Psalm 24:7

Send your light and truth.
They will escort me
to the holy mountain
where you make your home.
I will approach the altar of God,
God, my highest joy,
and praise you with the harp,
God, my God.

Psalm 43:3 – 4

People watched the procession
as you marched into your house,
my Lord, my sovereign God.
Singers at the head, musicians at the rear,
between them, women striking tambourines.

Psalm 68:25 – 26

Come, sing with joy to God,
shout to our savior, our rock.
Enter God's presence with praise,
enter with shouting and song.

Psalm 95:1– 2

Shout joy to the Lord, all earth,
serve the Lord with gladness,
enter God's presence with joy!
Know that the Lord is God,
our maker to whom we belong,
our shepherd, and we the flock.
Enter the temple gates,

the courtyard with thanks and praise;
give thanks and bless God's name.
Indeed the Lord is good!
God's love is for ever,
faithful from age to age.

Psalm 100

This is the day the Lord made,
let us rejoice and be glad.
Blest is the one who comes,
who comes in the name of the Lord.
We bless you from the Lord's house.
The Lord God is our light;
adorn the altar with branches.

Psalm 118:24, 26

Documentation

The purpose of this song is to open the celebration, intensify the unity of the gathered people, lead their thoughts to the mystery of the season or feast. . . .

***General Instruction of the Roman Missal,* 25**

The entrance rite should create an atmosphere of celebration. It serves the function of putting the assembly in the proper frame of mind for listening to the word of God. It helps people to become conscious of themselves as a worshiping community. The choice of texts for the entrance song should not conflict with these purposes.

***Appendix to the General Instruction,* 26**

The entrance song should create an atmosphere of celebration. It helps put the assembly in the proper frame of mind for listening to the Word of God. It helps people to become conscious of themselves as a worshiping community. The choice of texts for the entrance song should not conflict with these purposes.

***Music in Catholic Worship,* 61**

The entrance song serves to gather and unite the assembly and set the tone for the celebration.

***Liturgical Music Today,* 18**

Other Sources

The goal is not song, but prayer.

James Hansen

We sing our heritage and our present moment.

Nancy Chvatal

The purpose of music and text is not merely to affirm widely held values or to invoke participation. The purpose of song in the rite is to provoke a decision *(metanoia)* regarding our commitment to the values and person of Jesus of Nazareth and to one another.

Tom Conry

I do not desire you to please me; I do desire you to sing. Come, more; another stanzo: Call you 'em stanzos?

William Shakespeare

Pastoral musicians must learn to love the sound of a singing congregation above any other sound.

Charles Gardner

The main problem with using a processional . . . is that when there's a parade everyone loves to watch. . . . In fact, the too frequent use of a processional probably accounts for much of the lack of enthusiasm often heard during the opening song. . . . Read a hymn instead of watching the bride? Instead of watching a line of angelically dressed seven-year-olds? Are you kidding? No contest!

Elaine Rendler

We will never, as a church, mature in our hymn-singing experience until, among other things, we learn to sing hymns in their entirety.

Bob Batastini

We must remember that hymn singing is folk art. It is the people's music.

Frank Brownstead

We come to share our story,
we come to break the bread,
We come to know our rising from the dead.

David Haas

Gather us in — the lost and forsaken,
Gather us in — the blind and the lame,
Call to us now and we shall awaken,
We shall arise at the sound of our name.

Marty Haugen

What is this place where we are meeting?
Only a house, the earth its floor,
Walls and a roof, sheltering people,
Windows for light, an open door.
Yet it becomes a body that lives
When we are gathered here,
And know our God is near.

Huub Oosterhuis

Here the love of God, through Jesus,
Is revealed in time and space. . . .
Here the outcast and the strangers
bear the image of God's face. . . .
All are welcome,
all are welcome,
all are welcome in this place.

Marty Haugen

Background and Commentary

In many parishes, the cantor introduces the gathering song with "Let us stand and greet our celebrant," but that is actually a lie. The point of the gathering song is not to greet the celebrant or to provide traveling music for the priest. Rather, its purpose is to gather and galvanize the community — to greet *the Lord and each other,* not the presider. This is not to diminish the importance of the priest. But it is incorrect and dangerous to begin the liturgy with any message that implies that the priest is the point or the primary minister of the worship. The Lord is the center of our worship, and the entire baptized assembly, the body of Christ, is the primary agent and minister of the liturgy. The *General Instruction of the Roman Missal* gives us the direction for the introductory rites:

> The purpose of these rites is that the faithful coming together take on the form of a community and prepare themselves to listen to God's word and celebrate the eucharist properly. (24)

This coming together of the community is also the intent of the song of gathering. The best kind of music here is a piece in strophic hymn form, with the assembly singing the entire hymn or song. An anthem sung by the choir alone defeats the purpose of the moment. Refrain/verse arrangements can sometimes work well, but if the assembly is given a brief refrain while the real center of the song is in the glory of the verses sung by the cantor or choir, the song defeats the intention of the coming together of the community.

Similarly, many worshipers perceive the opening procession as the grand entrance of the priest, and the song as music to accompany his entrance, rather than as the first act of worship by the assembly. We musicians have been known to foster this perception. Usually we choose a three- or four-stanza hymn for this procession. The priest generally arrives at the presidential chair by the end of the second stanza. When we end the hymn there, we are suggesting very strongly that the hymn has completed its purpose. If we courageously sing all four stanzas of the hymn, the assembly (and sometimes the presider) may wonder why the music is continuing. If so, it is because we have trained them that the purpose of the hymn is to greet the celebrant.

How can we overcome this perception? There are many ways. For example, the priest should be part of the hospitality ministry before the formal celebration begins, in the gathering space (if there is one) or in the body of the worship space, welcoming and greeting the people of the community. The priest could then simply take his place when it is time to begin or, as some presiders choose to do, sit in one of the front pews among the assembly. Then the music rehearsal could take place, with the priest participating as well. After the rehearsal and some period of silence, he would stand up and move to the front. As instrumental music plays softly, he would lead the sign of the cross, offer the greeting and introduce the celebration. Then he and the assembly would sing the gathering song. This option makes clear that the priest is worshiping with everyone else; it also makes clear that the song of gathering is not traveling music, but rather the prayer of the assembly.

Another option is this: When there is a procession, choose a hymn that can be divided. Two or three stanzas are sung to accompany the procession, then the musicians play quietly while the presider proceeds with the sign of the cross and the greeting. Then the interlude crescendoes into the final stanzas of the hymn, sung by assembly, ministers and presider in place. The presider would then proceed with the rest of the gathering rites.

Whatever option is chosen, the gathering song must be experienced as prayer, a faith statement of this community coming to worship.

Sign of the Cross and Greeting

Scripture

I am the God of your father Abraham; do not be afraid, for I am with you and will bless you.

Genesis 26:24

Boaz came from Bethlehem. He said to the reapers, "The LORD be with you!" They answered, "The LORD bless you."

Ruth 2:4

"Greetings, favored one! The Lord is with you."

Luke 1:28

And the Word became flesh and lived among us, and we have seen his glory.

John 1:14

And remember, I am with you always, to the end of the age.

Matthew 28:20b

The grace of the Lord Jesus Christ, the love of God, and the communion of the Holy Spirit be with all of you.

2 Corinthians 13:13

May the grace of our Lord Jesus Christ be with your spirit, brothers and sisters. Amen.

Galatians 6:18

Grace to you and peace from God our Father and the Lord Jesus Christ.

Ephesians 1:2

The Lord be with your spirit. Grace be with you.

2 Timothy 4:22

See, the home of God is among mortals. He will dwell with them as their God; they will be his peoples, and God himself will be with them.

Revelation 21:3

Documentation

After the entrance song, the priest and the whole assembly make the sign of the cross. Then through his greeting the priest declares that the Lord is present. This greeting and the congregation's response express the mystery of the gathered Church.

General Instruction of the Roman Missal, 28

Other Sources

If you are tempted, hasten to sign yourselves on the forehead in a worthy manner. For this sign manifests the Passion which stands against the devil, provided you make it with faith. . . . Then the adversary, seeing the power that comes from the heart, will flee. . . . By signing . . . we repulse him who seeks to destroy us.

Apostolic Tradition

When we cross ourselves, let it be with a real sign of the cross. Instead of a small cramped gesture that gives no notion of its meaning, let us make a large unhurried sign, from forehead to breast, from shoulder to shoulder, consciously feeling how it includes the whole of us, our thoughts, our attitudes, our body and soul, every part of us at once, how it consecrates and sanctifies us. . . . It is the holiest of all signs. Make a large cross, taking time, thinking what you do. Let it take in your whole being — body, soul, mind, will, thoughts, feelings, your doing and not-doing — and by signing yourself with the cross strengthen and consecrate the whole in the strength of Christ, in the name of the triune God.

Romano Guardini

The reason for which some presidents choose to greet the assembly with "Good morning, everybody" instead of "The Lord be with you" is difficult to fathom.

Aidan Kavanagh

Background and Commentary

The sign of the cross is integral to the celebration of the eucharist, as it is whenever Christians gather. This trinitarian formula is a reminder of our baptism and a statement of our identity as the People of God. The greeting that follows is ancient and traditional to the Roman church. Its sources are found in many of the New Testament letters, and in the Old Testament Book of Ruth.

The greeting may be sung, and several musical settings are offered in the sacramentary. At present, this option is rarely used, if ever, in most communities. Many find it awkward to sing greetings, although some parishes follow this usage with great success.

The sacramentary suggests that an introduction to the liturgy may be made at this point, but it should be brief. This is not an opportunity for another homily.

Rite of Blessing and Sprinkling Holy Water

Scripture

Thus you shall do to them, to cleanse them: sprinkle the water of purification on them.

Numbers 8:7a

Wash me with fresh water,
wash me bright as snow.

Psalm 51:9

Bless God in the assembly,
all who draw water
from Israel's spring.

Psalm 68:27

Onward roll the waves, O God,
onward like thunder,
onward like fury.

Psalm 93:3

I will wash you in fresh water,
rid you from the filth of idols
and make you clean again.

Ezekiel 36:25

"Those who drink of the water that I will give them will never be thirsty. The water that I will give will become in them a spring of water gushing up to eternal life." The woman said to him, "Sir, give me this water, so that I may never be thirsty."

John 4:14–15a

Documentation

If Mass begins with the sprinkling of the people with blessed water, the penitential rite is omitted; this may be done at all Sunday Masses. (cf. RM, Blessing and Sprinkling of Holy Water, 1)

***Music in Catholic Worship*, 44**

This revised rite of sprinkling is no longer restricted to the principal Mass or to parish churches but may be used "at all Sunday Masses, even those anticipated on Saturday evening, in all churches and oratories." . . . [T]he selection of songs to accompany the sprinkling indicate[s] the purpose of the rite: to express the paschal character of Sunday and to be a memorial of baptism.

Foreword to the Sacramentary

Other Sources

Lord Jesus, from your wounded side
flowed streams of cleansing water: alleluia.

Roman Rite

Springs of water, bless the Lord!
Give God glory and praise forever.

Easter Vigil

God, you have moved upon the waters,
you have sung in the rush of wind and flame;
and in your love, you have called us sons and daughters,
make us people of the water and your name.

Marty Haugen

Water of life, Jesus our light,
Journey from death to new life.

David Haas

In the water we seek him,
in the wellspring of all that lives,
all who are thirsty,
come and be filled with the live he gives. . . .
Flowing out of the desert,
rolling down from the mountainside,
up from within you,
water of newness and life eternal.

Marty Haugen

Asperges me is not the same as, and much better than, "Sprinkle me."

Fred Moleck

Background and Commentary

After the sign of the cross and greeting the sacramentary offers several options, the first of which is the sprinkling rite. It is puzzling that this option is seldom used. Why is this? I am not sure. Perhaps Catholics would rather focus on their guilt than on their baptism and on their exalted status as adopted sons and daughters of the Lord.

The sprinkling rite expresses the baptismal call that we who gather to worship share in common; it is the continual renewal of our baptismal promises and mission. This option is permitted at all Sunday Masses, but is especially appropriate during the Easter season, particularly when baptisms are taking place. The Feast of the Baptism of the Lord, which concludes the Christmas season, is a celebration where the rite of sprinkling is an appropriate call to ministry.

The rite begins with an invitation to prayer and a period of silence, followed by a prayer of blessing over the water. This blessing could (and should) be done in a musical fashion, with the presider singing, chanting or proclaiming the blessing with acclamations or responses from the assembly. After the blessing, the presider then goes forth to sprinkle the assembly lavishly, so the people can actually feel the water. Music should accompany this entire action. There are many wonderful selections that work well with this moment. The Gloria might be sung during the sprinkling. If so, the opening prayer follows immediately.

Penitential Rite or Kyrie

Scripture

I will draw you from the nations,
gather you from exile
and bring you home.

Ezekiel 36:24

Happy the pardoned,
whose sin is canceled,
in whom God finds
no evil, no deceit.
Evil brings grief;
trusting in God brings love.

Psalm 32:2, 10a

Your mercy, Lord, spans the sky;
your faithfulness soars among the clouds.
Your integrity towers like a mountain;
your justice runs deeper than the sea.
Lord, you embrace all life:
How we prize your tender mercy!

Psalm 36:6 – 8

Have mercy, tender God,
forget that I defied you.
Wash away my sin,
cleanse me from my guilt.

Psalm 51:3 – 4

My soul, bless the Lord,
bless God's holy name!
My soul, bless the Lord,
hold dear all God's gifts!
Bless God, who forgives your sin
and heals every illness,
who snatches you from death
and enfolds you with tender care,
who fills your life with richness
and gives you an eagle's strength.
The Lord is tender and caring,
slow to anger, rich in love.
God will not accuse us long,
nor bring our sins to trial,
nor exact from us in kind
what our sins deserve.

Psalm 103:1– 5, 8 –10

Spare your people, O LORD.

Joel 2:17b

As Jesus went on . . . two blind men followed him, crying loudly, "Have mercy on us, Son of David!"

Matthew 9:27

Just then a Canaanite woman from that region came out and started shouting, "Have mercy on me, Lord, Son of David."

Matthew 15:22

As he and his disciples and a large crowd were leaving Jericho, Bartimaeus son of Timaeus, a blind beggar, was sitting by the roadside. When he heard that it was Jesus of Nazareth, he began to shout out and say, "Jesus, Son of David, have mercy on me!"

Mark 10:46 – 47

If God is for us, who is against us? . . . Who will bring any charge against God's elect? It is God who justifies. Who is to condemn? It is Christ Jesus, who died, yes, who was raised, who is at the right hand of God, who indeed intercedes for us. Who will separate us from the love of Christ? . . . I am convinced that neither death, nor life, nor angels, nor rulers, nor things present, nor things to come, nor powers, nor height, nor depth, nor anything else in all creation, will be able to separate us from the love of God in Christ Jesus our Lord.

Romans 8:31b, 33 – 35a, 38 – 39

Documentation

[After the penitential rite,] the Kyrie begins, unless it has already been included as part of the penitential rite. Since it is a song by which the faithful praise the Lord and implore his mercy, it is ordinarily prayed by all, that is, alternately by the congregation and the choir or cantor.

***General Instruction of the Roman Missal,* 30**

This short litany was traditionally a prayer of praise to the risen Christ. He has been raised and made "Lord," and we beg him to show his loving kindness. . . . When sung, the setting should be brief and simple in order not to give undue importance to the introductory rites.

***Music in Catholic Worship,* 65**

Other Sources

Hear us, almighty Lord,
show us your mercy,
Sinners we stand here before you.

Attende Domine

There's a wideness in God's mercy
like the wideness of the sea.

Frederick W. Faber

There is a balm in Gilead to make the wounded whole,
There is a balm in Gilead to heal the sin-sick soul.

African American spiritual

Let me taste your mercy like rain on my face.

Rory Cooney

Voices that challenge:
the healers who teach us forgiveness and mercy.

David Haas

Show us your mercy,
your mercy, harsh and lovely as the sea.

Rory Cooney

It is not so much a moment for asking forgiveness for our personal sins as for asking God to forgive our failure to live together as a sign to the world, as the Body of Christ.

Mark Searle

I'll give you a dollar for every word you leave out of the penitential rite.

Eugene Walsh

Background and Commentary

The penitential rite is a relatively recent development in the Roman Rite, and is one of the most misunderstood elements of the entire eucharistic celebration. This rite is not to be a list of our sins, nor is it to be an examination of our lives, such as the examination of conscience in the Rite of Penance. This rite remembers and rejoices in the unending mercy, compassion and goodness of God.

Like the sprinkling rite, this rite is optional. It is used in place of the sprinkling rite, not in addition to it. When used, the penitential rite should be adapted to the season or feast, or to the scriptural focus of the celebration.

The penitential rite begins with an address to the people, followed by a short period of silence. Then a plea for forgiveness takes place, taking one of three forms: (1) the Confiteor (I Confess) followed by a simple form of the Kyrie; (2) a short, dialogical prayer utilizing a single "Lord have mercy"; or (3) the full threefold Kyrie with christocentric invocations. The rite concludes with a prayer of absolution.

This part of the liturgy was never intended to be overtly penitential in character. In fact, when the Kyrie is used, it is most important that it be seen as an acclamation, not as a doleful self-accusation. The Greek "Kyrie eleison" is more an invocation of praise, honoring Christ as the one who reigns over the power and darkness of sin. Christ is greater than our sinfulness, greater than our hatred, our greed, our violence and abuse, our neglect, our racism, our addictions, all the things that we wish to be delivered from. Christ is the victor over all these things. The penitential rite should be an expression of this acknowledgment, for it is in that spirit that we come together to worship, to hear the reconciling and redeeming word of God, and to be nurtured and healed at the table of life.

There are many wonderful musical settings available that embody the true sense of this ritual moment, especially for the third, more litanic option of the penitential rite. There is ample room for creativity here. The many volumes of ritual music from the Taizé community (available from GIA Publications) are a good place to start exploring musical options. During Lent, a good musical setting of the Kyrie that has a clear litanic and processional character can serve as a processional and gathering song. This would give the beginning of the celebration a lenten focus. Using the Kyrie in this way would also keep the gathering rites from becoming too long.

No matter which options are chosen, the decision to sing any part of the penitential rite takes careful thinking through. There must be a clear purpose and intent for doing so. The penitential rite must be in balance with the entire gathering rite, and the rest of the celebration as well.

loria

Scripture

Glory to God in the highest heaven, and on earth peace among those whom he favors!

Luke 2:14

He destined us for adoption as his children through Jesus Christ, according to the good pleasure of his will, to the praise of his glorious grace that he freely bestowed on us in the Beloved. . . . In Christ we have also obtained an inheritance, having been destined according to the purpose of him who accomplishes all things according to his counsel and will, so that we, who were the first to set our hope on Christ, might live for the praise of his glory. . . . This is the pledge of our inheritance toward redemption as God's own people, to the praise of his glory.

Ephesians 1:5 – 6, 11–12, 14

It he alone who has immortality and dwells in unapproachable light, whom no one has ever seen or can see.

1 Timothy 6:16

Here is the Lamb of God who takes away the sin of the world!

John 1:29

So if you have been raised with Christ, seek the things that are above, where Christ is, seated at the right hand of God.

Colossians 3:1

Documentation

The Gloria is an ancient hymn in which the Church, assembled in the Holy Spirit, praises and entreats the Father and the Lamb. It is sung by the congregation, or by the congregation alternately with the choir, or by the choir alone. . . . The Gloria is sung or said on Sundays outside Advent and Lent, on solemnities and feasts, and in special, more solemn celebrations.

General Instruction of the Roman Missal, 31

The restricted use of the Gloria, i.e., only on Sundays outside Advent and Lent and on solemnities and feasts (GI, 31), emphasizes its special and solemn character. The new text offers many opportunities for alternation of choir and people in poetic parallelisms.

Music in Catholic Worship, 66

Other Sources

This ancient hymn . . . is an acclamation of God the Father and of his Christ, present among us who are members of his Body. The mood of the penitential rite and the mood of the Gloria are quite different, and it is hard to shift from the sobriety of the confession of sin to the exuberance of the Gloria without feeling forced. Generally speaking, it is better to chose either the penitential rite or the Gloria, rather than have both.

Mark Searle

Background and Commentary

The Gloria is an early Christian hymn. It is also known as the "angelic hymn," since its text is taken from the song the angels sang at Jesus' birth. Originally, the hymn was sung at Morning Prayer in the East. Eventually it was adopted in the West, first to be sung at Christmas, and later at Sunday celebrations when the bishop presided. It was not until the eleventh and twelfth centuries that it was introduced for all Sunday celebrations, except during Advent and Lent. The text of the Gloria beautifully blends praise, petition and the centrality of the Trinity.

The Gloria is a hymn and should be sung. That may be obvious, but in many communities, this principle has not taken root.

Admittedly, the Gloria as song does present problems. Pastorally, singing the Gloria lengthens a gathering rite that is already filled with too many elements. This is especially obvious when the choir or schola sings the Gloria alone, with no participation from the assembly (an option that I would never consider). Musically, the structure of the text is difficult for composers to match to melodic patterns accessible to the average assembly.

One solution to the first problem may be to limit the use of the Gloria, respecting its festive character and place. Many liturgists and musicians have suggested that the Gloria should be sung only during the festive seasons: Christmas (beginning with Christmas Eve and concluding with the celebration of the Baptism of the Lord) and Easter (beginning with Easter Vigil and culminating with Pentecost). Other celebrations where the Gloria would be welcome are Holy Thursday, Corpus Christi, Trinity Sunday and Christ the King. Otherwise the Gloria would be omitted.

Another possible solution would be to sing the Gloria outside its usual placement in the gathering rites; for example, as a processional or gathering song, as a song to accompany the sprinkling rite, or as a song of praise after the communion rite.

As a solution to the musical problem, a refrain-verse pattern works well. There are many such settings to choose from in many styles and from many publishers. Alexander Peloquin originated this format with his ground-breaking "Gloria of the Bells" from the 1970s.

It is good for a community to know this ritual text by heart, as well as others such as the Kyrie, eucharistic acclamations and Lamb of God. I strongly recommend that music ministers not burden the assembly with many different settings of the Gloria. Choose one or two versions that work well and will stand the test of time. The community will learn them well and participate eagerly and enthusiastically.

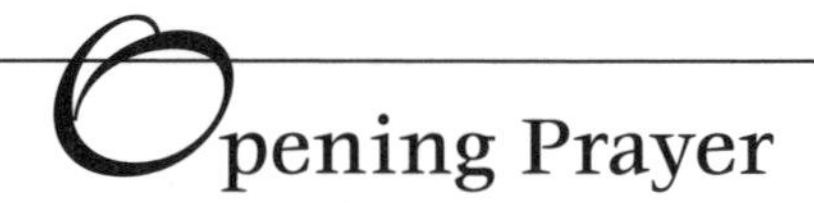

Opening Prayer

Scripture

Lord, I give myself to you.

Psalm 25:1

If in my name you ask me for anything, I will do it.

John 14:14

Pray without ceasing.

1 Thessalonians 5:17

He always lives to make intercession.

Hebrews 7:25b

And to the angel of the church . . . write: The words of the Amen, the faithful and true witness, the origin of God's creation.

Revelation 3:14

Documentation

The priest invites the people to pray and together with him they observe a brief silence so that they may realize they are in God's presence and may call their petitions to mind. . . . This expresses the theme of the celebration and the priest's words address a petition to God the Father through Christ in the Holy Spirit. The people make the prayer their own and give their assent by the acclamation, Amen.

***General Instruction of the Roman Missal,* 32**

The priest . . . addresses these prayers to God in the name of the entire holy people and all present. Thus there is good reason to call them "the presidential prayers."

***General Instruction of the Roman Missal,* 10**

Other Sources

I say "Yes," my Lord,
in all the good times,
through all the bad times . . .
to ev'ry word you speak.

Donna Peña

The only really indispensable part of the introductory rites is the collect, or the opening prayer. This is the point to which everything else leads, the point at which this crowd of people, who have just come from their homes or workplaces . . . can find themselves together as a community. . . . We come together now as the Body of Christ. We lost our individuality to find our common identity; we let the noise and preoccupations of our lives die away as we become aware of him in whose presence we stand, and of those with whom we stand.

Mark Searle

Background and Commentary

Along with the song of gathering, the most important part of the introductory rites is the opening prayer. This prayer truly brings together the assembly in the presence of the Lord and sets the prayerful tone for the entire liturgical celebration. This prayer is called a *collect* (from the Latin *collecta),* and it does just what it sounds like: It "collects" all the prayers of the community into a unified whole, and prepares us to encounter God's word.

Notes

chapter TWO

The Liturgy of the Word

General Background

Scripture

O mortal, eat what is offered to you; eat this scroll, and go, speak to the house of Israel.

Ezekiel 3:1

Then he said to me: Prophesy to these bones, and say to them: O dry bones, hear the word of the LORD.

Ezekiel 37:4

The Lord's word is pure,
like silver from the furnace,
seven times refined.

Psalm 12:7

All that I am longs for you,
I wait for your word.
I never forget your word,
for it is my life.
I am yours, save me!
I study your precepts.
You word is a lamp for my steps,
a light for my path.

Psalm 119:81, 93 – 94, 105

Every word of God proves true.

Proverbs 30:5a

My mother and my brothers are those who hear the word of God and do it.

Luke 8:21

Were not our hearts burning within us while he was talking to us on the road, while he was opening the scriptures to us?

Luke 24:32

When they had prayed, the place in which they were gathered together was shaken; and they were all filled with the Holy Spirit and spoke the word of God with boldness.

Acts 4:31

Take the helmet of salvation, and the sword of the Spirit, which is the word of God.

Ephesians 6:17

Remember Jesus Christ, raised from the dead, a descendant of David — that is my gospel, for which I suffer hardship, even to the point of being chained like a criminal. But the word of God is not chained.

2 Timothy 2:8 – 9

You have been born anew, not of perishable but of imperishable seed, through the living and enduring word of God.

1 Peter 1:23

Documentation

Sacred Scripture is of the greatest importance in the celebration of the liturgy. For it is from Scripture that the readings are given and explained in the homily and that psalms are sung; the prayers, collects, and liturgical songs are scriptural in their inspiration; it is from the Scriptures that actions and signs derive their meaning. . . . It is essential to promote that warm and living love for Scripture to which the venerable tradition of both Eastern and Western rites gives testimony.

Constitution on the Sacred Liturgy, 24

The treasures of the Bible are to be opened up more lavishly, so that a richer share in God's word may be provided for the faithful.

Constitution on the Sacred Liturgy, 51

When the Scriptures are read in the Church, God himself is speaking to his people, and Christ, present in his own word, is proclaiming the Gospel.

General Instruction of the Roman Missal, 9

Christ is present to the faithful through his own word. Through the chants the people make God's word their own.

General Instruction of the Roman Missal, 33

The readings lay the table of God's word for the faithful and open up the riches of the Bible to them. . . . By tradition the reading of the Scripture is a ministerial, not a presidential function.

General Instruction of the Roman Missal, 34

Sometimes, moreover, if the place itself and the nature of the community permit, it will be appropriate to celebrate the liturgy of the word, including a homily, with the children in a separate, but not too distant, room. Then, before the eucharistic liturgy begins, the children are led to the place where the adults have meanwhile celebrated their own liturgy of the word.

Directory for Masses with Children, 17

Readings from scripture are at the heart of the liturgy of the word. The homily, responsorial psalms, profession of faith, and general intercessions develop and complete it. . . . Christ is present through his word. . . . The chants and the profession of faith comprise the people's acceptance of God's Word. It is of primary importance that the people hear God's message of love, digest it with the aid of psalms, silence, and the homily, and respond, involving themselves in the great covenant of love and redemption. All else is secondary.

Music in Catholic Worship, 45

The word constantly proclaimed in the liturgy is always, then, a living, active word through the power of the Holy Spirit. It expresses the Father's love that never fails in its effectiveness toward us.

Lectionary for Mass: Introduction, 4

Other Sources

Ignorance of the Scriptures is ignorance of Christ.

Jerome

The memoirs of the apostles or the writings of the prophets are read for as long as time allows.

Justin Martyr

O Word ever springing forth,
measureless Duration,
eternal Light,
Fountain of mercy,
Worker of virtue
so that the singers of God
can live a holy life!

Clement of Alexandria

The Bible is intended to bring us into closer communion with God. It has that power, being something alive and full of energy. It can penetrate deeper than any two-edged sword, reaching the very division between soul and spirit. It can do that only if it is read, however, and read in something of the sequence and development in which it was written. The church's public prayer recognizes no source of suitable converse with God higher than the inspired books.

Gerard Sloyan

The reader who is not a living embodiment of fidelity to God's word has no business taking the lectern.

Ralph Keifer

As listeners, the members of the assembly are ministers of the Word.

Anthony Krisak

It is a concelebration of the word, involving lay ministries, the whole people, deacon and presider. It welcomes not simply God's words, but the God who has a word for us.

Ralph Keifer

Words from afar, stars that are falling,
Sparks that are sown in us like seed.
Names for our God, dreams, signs, and wonders
Sent from the past are all we need.

We in this place remember and speak
Again what we have heard:
God's free redeeming word.

Huub Oosterhuis

Background and Commentary

Before the Second Vatican Council, most Catholics did not place much emphasis on reading the Bible. We focused on the sacraments, particularly the eucharist. What most of us knew of the Bible were just the parts that were read at Mass: parts of some epistles and the Gospel of Matthew. Since the Council, we have begun to understand scripture as an essential part of our faith. However, the proclamation of the word of God has been part of the eucharistic celebration since very early in the history of the church, within a few years of the resurrection.

Our life of faith is a response to the good news of Jesus Christ. The proclamation of that good news is integral to any liturgical celebration; through it, Christ is present, revealing himself and drawing us to himself. The liturgy of the word, then, is not a mere introduction or prelude to the liturgy of the eucharist. It is equal in dignity to the liturgy of the eucharist. The ambo, the place from which the word is proclaimed (also called the pulpit) is the table of God's word. From it we are fed, just as we are from the altar.

The Lectionary The lectionary is the book from which the readings are proclaimed. The readings are organized according to a three-year cycle. Each year, the whole of the paschal mystery story is recounted. For each Sunday, three scripture readings are assigned. There is also a responsorial psalm proclaimed each Sunday. Psalms are also from scripture, so there are actually four proclamations of scripture each Sunday. In Year A the gospel readings are chosen primarily from Matthew; Year B uses the gospel of Mark as its main source (with a long series of readings from John's gospel during Ordinary Time); and the Year C gospels come mostly from Luke.

The lectionary is an important sign of Christ's presence in the word. It should be beautiful and dignified. Missalettes or sheets of paper never substitute for a lectionary in the ambo, nor do the workbooks that many lectors use to prepare for their ministry. The proclamation of the word of God is a dramatic event where the word is experienced at a deep level of consciousness; it is not a group reading exercise. The word is to be heard and listened to, not followed along with. For this reason, lectors are encouraged to prepare and to practice their readings, and members of the assembly are discouraged from using missalettes or other books containing the readings.

Liturgy of the Word for Children A separate liturgy of the word for children, in a place apart from the primary worship space, is celebrated in many parishes, often with great success. After the opening prayer, usually, the children come forward with a catechist to receive a blessing from the presider. They are then sent forth with a song or acclamation. After their celebration of the word, they return to the primary gathering just before or during the preparation of the gifts.

The purpose of such celebrations was articulated in the *Directory for Masses with Children:* to enable children to participate well and fully. It is important to remember that the "children's liturgy of the word" is liturgy. It is not to be a catechetical session or a time for play, no matter how educational or Bible-centered. The same requirements of every liturgy of the word apply here: Music, processions, strong symbols and a homily should always be included.

Liturgy of the Word and Music For musicians and planners, the liturgy of the word provides direction for each particular celebration. The word determines the focus of the celebration. In planning music for a celebration, take time to reflect prayerfully on the readings, especially the gospel reading and the first reading, as they are usually related in message and content. The psalm and the second reading come next. The readings provide a center (not a "theme") for the entire celebration — for music, homily, ritual choreography, environment: in other words, every aspect of the liturgy. A good scripture commentary or two should be kept next to your lectionary, sacramentary, hymnal and other musical resources. See the end of this chapter for suggestions.
The elements of the liturgy of the word are:

First Reading
Silence
Responsorial Psalm
Second Reading
Silence
Gospel Acclamation
Gospel
Homily
Silence
Profession of Faith
General Intercessions

Silence is an important element in the liturgy of the word. A period of silence follows the first two readings and the homily so that the scriptural message may take root in the heart of each hearer.

The responsorial psalm follows the silence after the first reading. Each Sunday has a proper psalm assigned, and there is always the pastoral option of using a common seasonal psalm.

The second reading is from the Christian scriptures, either from one of the letters (epistles) or from the Book of Revelation. During the Advent–Christmas period and the Lent–Easter period, the second readings are thematically linked to the other readings. In Ordinary Time, they are semi-continuous readings from various epistles.

The climax of the liturgy of the word is the proclamation of the gospel.

First Reading

Scripture

Moses came and told the people all the words of the LORD and all the ordinances; and all the people answered with one voice, and said, "All the words that the LORD has spoken we will do."

Exodus 24:3

We have heard the story
our ancestors told us
of your deeds so long ago.

Psalm 44:2

Listen, my people,
mark each word.
I begin with a story,
I speak of mysteries
welling up from ancient depths,
heard and known from our elders.

We must not hide
this story from our children
but tell the mighty works
and all the wonders of God.
The Lord gave precepts to Jacob,
instructions to Israel,
that the people before us
could teach their children.

Let future generations learn
and let them grow up
to teach their young
to trust in God,
remembering great deeds,
cherishing the law.

Psalm 78:1–5

Documentation

The wonderful works of God among the people of the Old Testament were a prelude to the work of Christ the Lord.

***Constitution on the Sacred Liturgy,* 5**

After the opening prayer, the reader goes to the lectern for the first reading.

***General Instruction of the Roman Missal,* 89**

Each Mass has three readings: the first from the Old Testament. . . . This arrangement brings out the unity of the Old and New Testaments and of the history of salvation, in which Christ is the central figure, commemorated in his paschal mystery.

Lectionary for Mass: Introduction, 66, no. 1

The present Order of Readings selects Old Testament texts mainly because of their correlation with New Testament texts read at the same Mass, and particularly with the Gospel text. . . . The Old Testament reading is harmonized with the Gospel.

Lectionary for Mass: Introduction, 67

Other Sources

The Old Testament reading . . . gives us a sense of perspective, a perspective which does not end with the Gospel but which runs from the past, through the present, and into the future. The Old Testament readings on Sundays and during the seasons of Advent, Lent and Easter always have some connection with the gospel.

Mark Searle

Background and Commentary

The first reading on Sunday is always from the Hebrew scriptures, except during the Easter season, when the first readings are taken from the Acts of the Apostles. The presence of readings from the Old Testament in the liturgy of the word is a wonderful result of the liturgical reform. This reading serves as a partner to the gospel reading, and reveals to us God's activity in relationship to us throughout time. This is why we continue to tell these old stories — because they become new and real for us in the everyday situations of our lives. These readings from the Old Testament provide an element of pastoral care found nowhere else. The struggles of the ancients are the same struggles that we face. We need these stories; our concept of the "People of God" has its roots in them. These stories teach us and help us remember who we are.

Many of the Old Testament offerings in the lectionary are musical canticles, such as the Exodus canticle which is read at the Easter Vigil. At special times, presenting these canticles in a musical arrangement can be very effective.

ilence

Documentation

Silence should be observed at the designated times as part of the celebration. Its function depends on the time it occurs in each part of the celebration. . . . At . . . the conclusion of a reading . . . all meditate briefly on what has been heard.

General Instruction of the Roman Missal, 23

It is of primary importance that the people hear God's message of love, digest it with the aid of psalms [and] silence.

Music in Catholic Worship, 45

To facilitate reflection, there may be a brief period of silence between the first reading and the responsorial psalm.

Music in Catholic Worship, 63

The liturgy of the word must be celebrated in a way that fosters meditation; clearly, any sort of haste that hinders recollection must be avoided. The dialogue between God and his people taking place through the Holy Spirit demands short intervals of silence, suited to the assembled congregation, as an opportunity to take the word of God to heart and to prepare a response to it in prayer. Proper times for silence during the liturgy of the word are . . . after the first and the second reading.

Lectionary for Mass: Introduction, 28

Other Sources

Twofold is the meaning of silence. One, the abstinence from speech, the absence of sound. Two, inner silence, the absence of self concern, stillness. One may articulate words with the voice and yet be inwardly silent. One may abstain from uttering any sound and yet be overbearing.

Abraham Joshua Heschel

Background and Commentary

Silence in liturgical celebrations is difficult, and difficult to discuss. We tend to feel uncomfortable with keeping quiet in communal worship, so we do it badly. The liturgy calls for intentional silence at various times in the liturgy; the most important of these are the times between the readings during the liturgy of the word. The lector can help direct this silence by remaining at the ambo, still and silent, for a period of time. Once the silence has taken hold, the lector may be seated, joining the assembly in reflection and meditation on what they have just heard.

Responsorial Psalm

Scripture

It was the duty of trumpeters and singers to make themselves heard in unison in praise and thanksgiving to the LORD, and when the song was raised, with trumpets and cymbals and other musical instruments, in praise to the LORD, "For he is good, for his steadfast love endures forever," the house, the house of the LORD, was filled with a cloud, so that the priests could not stand to minister because of the cloud; for the glory of the LORD filled the house of God.

2 Chronicles 5:13–14

Listen today to God's voice:
Harden no heart.

Psalm 95:8

This is what counts for me:
to obey your commands.
Lord, my part
is to keep your word.
I pray from my heart,
remember your promise of mercy.

Psalm 119:56–58

These are my words that I spoke to you while I was still with you — that everything written about me in the law of Moses, the prophets, and the psalms must be fulfilled.

Luke 24:44

Be filled with the Spirit, as you sing psalms and hymns and spiritual songs among yourselves, singing and making melody to the Lord in your hearts, giving thanks to God the Father at all times and for everything in the name of our Lord Jesus Christ.

Ephesians 5:18b–20

Documentation

[The psalm is] an integral part of the liturgy of the word. . . . The texts are directly connected with the individual readings. . . . In order that the people may be able to join in . . . more easily, some texts of psalms have been chosen, according to the different seasons of the years and classes of saints, for optional use, whenever the psalm is sung, instead of the text corresponding to the reading. . . . The cantor of the psalm sings the verses of the psalm at the lectern or other suitable place. The people . . . take part by singing the response.

***General Instruction of the Roman Missal,* 36**

The choice of texts that are *not* from the psalter . . . is not extended to the chants between the readings. . . . In particular, see the common texts for sung responsorial psalms (nos. 174–175), which may be used in place of the text corresponding to the reading whenever the psalm is sung.

Appendix to the General Instruction, 36

It is of primary importance that the people hear God's message of love [and] digest it with the aid of psalms.

Music in Catholic Worship, 45

This unique and very important song is the response to the first lesson. . . . The liturgy of the Word comes more fully to life if between the first two readings a cantor sings the psalm and all sing the response. Since most groups cannot learn a new response every week, seasonal refrains are offered in the lectionary itself. . . . The choice of the texts which are not from the psalter is not extended to the chants between the readings (NCCB, Nov. 1968, cf. GI, 6).

Music in Catholic Worship, 63

The psalms and canticles are songs; therefore they are most satisfying when sung.

Liturgical Music Today, 35

The faithful must be continually instructed on the way to perceive the word of God speaking in the psalms and to turn these psalms into the prayer of the Church.

Lectionary for Mass: Introduction, 19

As a rule the responsorial psalm should be sung.

Lectionary for Mass: Introduction, 20

The singing of the psalm, or even of the response alone, is a great help toward understanding and meditating on the psalm's spiritual meaning. To foster the congregation's singing, every means available in each individual culture is to be employed. In particular, use is to be made of all the relevant options provided in the Order of Readings for Mass regarding responses corresponding to the different liturgical seasons.

Lectionary for Mass: Introduction, 21

The responsorial psalm is sung or recited by the psalmist or cantor at the ambo.

Lectionary for Mass: Introduction, 22

Other Sources

What is more pleasing than a psalm? David himself puts it nicely: "Praise the Lord," he says, "for a psalm is good" (Psalm 146:1). And indeed! A psalm is the blessing of the people, the praise of God, the commendation of the multitude, the applause of all, the speech of every person, the voice of the church, the sonorous profession of faith, devotion full of authority, the joy of liberty, the noise of good cheer, and the echo of gladness. It softens anger, it gives release from anxiety, it alleviates sorrow; it is protection at night, instruction by day, a shield in time of fear, a feast of holiness, the image of tranquillity, a pledge of peace and harmony, which produces one song from various and sundry voices in the manner of a cithara. The day's dawning resounds with a psalm, with a psalm its passing echoes.

Ambrose

Background and Commentary

The singing of the responsorial psalm follows the ancient Jewish synagogue practice of the community responding to the scripture reading with a psalm or a biblical canticle. This text used to be called the *gradual,* after the place where it was proclaimed: the *gradus,* the steps of the altar.

The responsorial psalm is always to be sung. Not to sing the psalm would be the same as reciting "Happy Birthday," which, of course, is ludicrous. The psalms are lyrical and musical in intent. The responsorial form and function of this sung proclamation readily lend themselves to the refrain-verse format of rendition, but there are settings in strophic or metrical forms — hymns — that serve the text well. These should be considered occasionally.

A Proclamation of Scripture The responsorial psalm is often treated as a sort of musical intermission between the readings, which is a misunderstanding. In reality, the psalm is the "second reading"; it is scripture proclamation in its own right. This is why the *General Instruction* recommends that the psalm be proclaimed from the ambo, giving it the dignity it deserves as the word of God.

This particular scripture reading is proclaimed by the gathered assembly in their singing of the refrain, or antiphon. The role of the assembly is more than attentive listening; it is active proclamation, in dialogue with the cantor and other music ministers. When we liberate the responsorial psalm from being seen as a mere response to the first reading, we see it as an integral part of the liturgy of the word, in relationship and unity with the other scripture readings of the liturgy. The word "responsorial" refers more to its form and structure than to its role.

Nothing other than a psalm will do in this situation. A nice song, however meaningful, is not appropriate unless it is an actual psalm setting. A song that quotes a line or two from a psalm text is not enough. Within the psalter we find every conceivable human condition and situation. All the many journeys of the human spirit are found here: joy, praise, ecstasy, hope, promise, fear, loneliness, anger and even rage. Why would we need to look elsewhere? The Book of Psalms is perhaps the most human — and therefore most pastoral — book in the Bible. It is unfortunate that homilists often overlook the psalm text in their preaching; these verses often provide a pastoral link to good evangelization, catechesis and mystagogy.

Proper and Common Psalms Musicians and liturgists should attend to the *proper* psalm, that is, the one assigned to a particular Sunday or sacramental celebration. The lectionary also offers the option of using seasonal, or *common* psalms: texts that may be used throughout a season.

The use of common psalmody has certain positive aspects. A particular assembly may find it easier to learn one musical setting of a particular text, and its familiarity over time may invite participation. In certain pastoral settings, I have found this option helpful. It is particularly effective with an assembly that is still finding its voice, not yet used to participating in sung psalmody. I have also found that using a common responsorial psalm throughout a season can help unify that season without being an artificially imposed theme.

It is important, however, to move beyond this practice after a while, and strive to use the proper psalms given to us in the lectionary. This will enrich the entire liturgy of the word. It will also help us become more biblically literate, and help us explore the treasures of these ancient, sacred prayers.

Second Reading

Scripture

Indeed, the word of God is living and active, sharper than any two-edged sword, piercing until it divides soul from spirit, joints from marrow; it is able to judge the thoughts and intentions of the heart.

Hebrews 4:12

Be doers of the word, and not merely hearers who deceive themselves. For if any are hearers of the word and not doers, they are like those who look at themselves in a mirror; for they look at themselves, and, on going away, immediately forget what they were like. But those who look into the perfect law, the law of liberty, and persevere, being not hearers who forget but doers who act — they will be blessed in their doing.

James 1:22 – 25

Documentation

Then, if there is a second reading before the gospel, the reader reads it at the lectern as before.

General Instruction of the Roman Missal, 91

The doctrine and events recounted in texts of the New Testament bear a more or less explicit relationship to the doctrine and events of the Old Testament. . . . The text of both the apostolic and Gospel readings are arranged in order of semicontinuous reading, whereas the Old Testament reading is harmonized with the Gospel.

Lectionary for Mass: Introduction, 67

Other Sources

Frequently the second reading at Sunday Mass is difficult to "connect" with the other two. This is because it is selected on a different principle. . . . The second reading, usually from the epistles, is part of a continuous reading of a particular book. Sometimes it does shed light on the other two readings, but sometimes it is on a different track completely, and many people find this confusing. . . . Sometimes it might be better to omit it altogether. The rubrics permit this for "pastoral reasons," and I would think that the causing of confusion would be a good pastoral reason.

Mark Searle

Background and Commentary

The second reading can be difficult pastorally in its relationship to the other biblical readings at liturgy. The second readings are chosen according to a different system and logic. Often these readings are semi-continuous, except during the major liturgical seasons, when a certain relationship can be established with the first reading and the gospel. It is recommended that there be two lectors at any celebration, so that the first and second readings may be heard in different ways.

The second reading often is a help to music ministers in their planning of music. Many of these passages are Christological hymns or texts that have been set to music, especially by contemporary liturgical composers.

Gospel Acclamation

Scripture

Hallelujah!
How good to sing God praise!
How lovely the sound!

Psalm 147:1

Hallelujah!
Praise the Lord!
Across the heavens,
from the heights,
all you angels, heavenly beings,
sing praise, sing praise!

Psalm 148:1–2

Hallelujah!
Sing a new song, you faithful,
praise God in the assembly.

Psalm 149:1

Praise! Praise God with . . . dance . . .
All that is alive, praise. Praise the Lord.
Hallelujah!

Psalm 150:4, 6

Hallelujah! For the Lord our God the Almighty reigns.

Revelation 19:6b

Documentation

The Alleluia is sung in every season outside Lent. It is begun either by all present or by the choir or cantor; it may then be repeated. The verses are taken from the Lectionary or the *Graduale.*

***General Instruction of the Roman Missal,* 37**

If not sung, the Alleluia or the verse before the gospel may be omitted.

***General Instruction of the Roman Missal,* 39**

During Lent the alleluia is not sung with the verse before the Gospel. Instead one of the following (or similar) acclamations may be sung before and after the verse before the Gospel:

Praise and honor to you, Lord Jesus Christ, King of endless glory!
Praise and honor to you, Lord Jesus Christ!
Glory and praise to you, Lord Jesus Christ!
Glory to you, Word of God, Lord Jesus Christ!

***Appendix to the General Instruction,* 36**

The acclamations are shouts of joy which arise from the whole assembly as forceful and meaningful assents to God's Word and Action. They are important because they make some of the most significant moments of the Mass . . . stand out. It is of their nature that they be rhythmically strong, melodically appealing, and affirmative. The people should know the acclamations by heart in order to sing them spontaneously.

Music in Catholic Worship, 53

This acclamation of paschal joy is both a reflection upon the Word of God proclaimed in the liturgy and a preparation for the gospel. All stand to sing it. After the cantor or choir sings the alleluia(s), the people customarily repeat it. Then a single proper verse is sung by the cantor or choir, and all repeat the alleluia(s). If not sung, the alleluia should be omitted (GI, 39). A moment of silent reflection may be observed in its place. During Lent a brief verse of acclamatory character replaces the alleluia and is sung in the same way.

Music in Catholic Worship, 55

The acclamations . . . are the preeminent sung prayers of the eucharistic liturgy. Singing these acclamations makes their prayer all the more effective. . . . The gospel acclamation, moreover, must always be sung (LMIn, 23).

Liturgical Music Today, 17

The Alleluia, or, as the liturgical season requires, the verse before the gospel, is also a "rite or act standing by itself." It serves as the greeting of welcome of the assembled faithful to the Lord who is about to speak to them and as an expression of their faith through song. The Alleluia or the verse before the Gospel must be sung and during it all stand. It is not to be sung only by the cantor who intones it or by the choir, but by the whole of the people together.

Lectionary for Mass: Introduction, 23

During Lent one of the acclamations from those given in the Order of Readings may be used, depending on the occasion. This acclamation precedes and follows the verse before the Gospel.

Lectionary for Mass: Introduction, 91

Other Sources

Stand up friends!
Hold your heads high!
Freedom is our song, Alleluia!

Brian Wren

How can a shout be sung?

Miriam Therese Winter

Background and Commentary

The word "alleluia" has its origins in the Hebrew scriptures. It basically means, "Praise God." We find this word often in the psalter. As time went on, it became part of Christian worship as a song of joy for the celebrations of Easter. Since every liturgical celebration is a proclamation of the resurrection, of the risen Lord, "alleluia" is at the heart of Christian worship.

The role and intent of the gospel acclamation is completely different from those of the responsorial psalm. First of all, it is an acclamation. The responsorial psalm exists for its own sake, one could say; it does not lead from or to something else. The gospel acclamation, however, is not its own moment, nor does it depend on something that preceded it. It is anticipatory. It should relentlessly direct the assembly's attention to the gospel proclamation that follows. This means that not every musical piece that includes the word "alleluia" is necessarily a good gospel acclamation.

The gospel acclamation must have strong rhythmic vitality and energy, although it does not have to be fast. It must be led with strength. Acclamations are not mere assent; rather, they should express an investment on the part of the assembly. Many acclamations fail to do this. The gospel acclamation is always sung. It is more important to sing the gospel acclamation and the other primary acclamations (Holy, Holy, memorial acclamation, and Great Amen) than the opening and closing hymns. The acclamations are the moments when the assembly takes seriously its role, not just singing at the liturgy, but rather, "singing the liturgy."

Processional Music The gospel acclamation is processional music. It accompanies the procession of the gospel book and its proclaimer to the ambo. The length of the gospel acclamation is determined by the time necessary to complete the ritual action. The one who is to proclaim the gospel should be moving during the singing; the ritual dialogue (The Lord be with you / And also with you) begins immediately upon the completion of the acclamation. Any other gestures (taking up the book, incensing the book and ambo, blessing of the deacon, etc.) should take place during the music, not afterward in silence. If the music is not long enough to accompany these actions, the musician should lengthen the acclamation or add additional verses, or the gestures should be reconsidered.

Should the acclamation be repeated after the gospel proclamation? We need to remember "alleluia" means "praise the Lord." What do we usually say (usually lethargically) at the end of the gospel? "Praise to you, Lord Jesus Christ." Repeating the sung acclamation at the end of the gospel reading would be in keeping with the spirit of the assembly's response, and may be more clearly emphatic and passionate than the usual murmured response.

Proclamation of the Gospel

Scripture

For I am not ashamed of the gospel; it is the power of God for salvation to everyone who has faith.

Romans 1:16a

Our message of the gospel came to you not in word only, but also in power and in the Holy Spirit and with full conviction.

1 Thessalonians 1:5a

For this purpose he called you through our proclamation of the good news, so that you may obtain the glory of our Lord Jesus Christ.

2 Thessalonians 2:14

Long ago God spoke to our ancestors in many and various ways by the prophets, but in these last days he has spoken to us by a Son, whom he appointed heir of all things, through whom he also created the worlds. He is the reflection of God's glory and the exact imprint of God's very being, and he sustains all things by his powerful word.

Hebrews 1:1–3

Documentation

It is Christ himself who speaks when the Holy Scriptures are read in the Church.

Constitution on the Sacred Liturgy, 7

The liturgy itself inculcates the great reverence to be shown toward the reading of the gospel, setting it off from the other readings by special marks of honor. . . . The people, who by their acclamations acknowledge and confess that Christ is present and speaking to them, stand as they listen to it.

General Instruction of the Roman Missal, 35

Of all the rites connected with the liturgy of the word, the reverence due to the Gospel reading must receive special attention.

Lectionary for Mass: Introduction, 17

Background and Commentary

The entire liturgy of the word is a celebration and proclamation of God's living presence with us, but the gospel reading crystallizes this presence, and is the obvious high point of this biblical sharing: The gospel is the Christ proclaimed in our midst. This is why the gospel acclamation is accompanied by procession, song, candles and incense. This is also why a separate beautiful book of the gospels is often used. The proclamation of the gospel is a most holy moment, and deserves all the care and preparation we can provide.

Musically and dramatically, there is much room for creativity here, but caution must be taken not to turn the reading into a historical re-enactment. This sometimes happens with dramatic renditions of the Passion reading on Passion Sunday and Good Friday, and in other celebrations of the Triduum, and also at Christmastime. However, many published resources offer good dramatic renderings, using elements of "readers' theater" and other narrative genres, sometimes employing a group of readers, sometimes interspersing musical acclamations or interventions throughout (especially for the gospel readings for the scrutinies during Lent, and for proclamations of the Passion). There is the historic tradition of singing or chanting the gospel reading, which can be very effective.

Homily

Scripture

Now the LORD came and stood there, calling as before, "Samuel! Samuel!" And Samuel said, "Speak, for your servant is listening."

1 Samuel 3:10

So they read from the book, from the law of God, with interpretation. They gave the sense, so that the people understood the reading.

Nehemiah 8:8

For as the rain and the snow come down from heaven, and do not return there until they have watered the earth, making it bring forth and sprout, giving seed to the sower and bread to the eater, so shall my word be that goes out from my mouth; it shall not return to me empty, but it shall accomplish that which I purpose, and succeed in the thing for which I sent it.

Isaiah 55:10 –11

"Yes," I said, "I will come
to live by your written word."
I want to do what pleases you;
your teaching is in my heart.

Psalm 40:8 – 9

And he rolled up the scroll, gave it back to the attendant, and sat down. The eyes of all in the synagogue were fixed on him. Then he began to say to them, "Today this scripture has been fulfilled in your hearing." All spoke well of him and were amazed at the gracious words that came from his mouth.

Luke 4:20 – 22a

Were not our hearts burning within us while he was talking to us on the road, while he was opening the scriptures to us?

Luke 24:31b

How are they to believe in one of whom they have never heard? And how are they to hear without someone to proclaim him?

Romans 10:14

But we speak God's wisdom, secret and hidden, which God decreed before the ages for our glory.

1 Corinthians 2:7

When you received the word of God that you heard from us, you accepted it not as a human word but as what it really is, God's word.

1 Thessalonians 2:13b

Remember your leaders, those who spoke the word of God to you; consider the outcome of their way of life, and imitate their faith. Jesus Christ is the same yesterday and today and forever.

Hebrews 13:7–8

Whoever speaks must do so as one speaking the very words of God.

1 Peter 4:11

Documentation

The ministry of preaching is to be fulfilled with exactitude and fidelity. Preaching should draw its content mainly from scriptural and liturgical sources, being a proclamation of God's wonderful works in the history of salvation, the mystery of Christ, ever present and active within us, especially in the celebration of the liturgy.

Constitution on the Sacred Liturgy, 35, no. 2

By means of the homily the mysteries of the faith and guiding principles of the Christian life are expounded from the sacred text during the course of the liturgical year.

Constitution on the Sacred Liturgy, 52

The homily is . . . an integral part of the liturgy and . . . necessary for the nurturing of the Christian life. It should develop some point of the readings or of another text from the Ordinary or the Proper of the Mass of the day, and take into account the mystery that is being celebrated and the needs proper to the listeners.

General Instruction of the Roman Missal, 41

Through the course of the liturgical year the homily sets forth the mysteries of faith and the standards of the Christian life on the basis of the sacred text. . . . It must always lead the community of the faithful to celebrate the Eucharist actively. . . . This demands that the homily be truly the fruit of meditation, carefully prepared, neither too long nor too short, and suited to all those present, even children and the uneducated.

Lectionary for Mass: Introduction, 24

Any necessary announcements are to be kept completely separate from the homily.

Lectionary for Mass: Introduction, 27

With the consent of the pastor or rector of the church, one of the adults may speak to the children after the gospel, especially if the priest finds it difficult to adapt himself to the mentality of children.

Directory for Masses with Children, 24

The homily explaining the word of God should be given great prominence in all Masses with children. Sometimes the homily intended for children should become a dialogue with them, unless it is preferred that they should listen in silence.

Directory for Masses with Children, 48

Unless a preacher knows what a congregation needs, wants, or is able to hear, there is every possibility that the message offered in the homily will not meet the needs of the people who hear it. To say this is by no means to imply that preachers are only to preach what their congregations want to hear. Only when preachers know what their congregations want to hear will they be able to communicate what a congregation needs to hear.

Fulfilled in Your Hearing, 4

Through words drawn from the Scriptures, from the church's theological tradition, and from the personal appropriation of that tradition through study and prayer, the preacher joins himself and the congregation in a common vision. We can say, therefore, that the homily is a unifying moment in the celebration of the liturgy, deepening and giving expression to the unity that is already present through the sacrament of baptism.

Fulfilled in Your Hearing, 11

Like all preaching, the homily is directed to faith.

Fulfilled in Your Hearing, 41

A homily presupposes faith. . . . The homily is preached in order that a community of believers who have gathered to celebrate the liturgy may do so more deeply and more fully — more faithfully — and thus be formed for Christian witness in the world. . . .56

Fulfilled in Your Hearing, 43

The homily is not so much *on* the Scriptures as *from* and *through* them.

Fulfilled in Your Hearing, 50

The goal of the liturgical preacher is not to interpret a text of the Bible (as would be the case in teaching a Scripture class) as much as to draw on the texts of the Bible as they are presented in the lectionary to interpret peoples' lives.

Fulfilled in Your Hearing, 52

The preparation for a Sunday homily should begin early in the week whenever possible, even on Sunday evening.

Fulfilled in Your Hearing, 86

The presiding minister is a person of the "Book" (the Scriptures), whose role is to articulate the tale of the Christ event so that people can relate the salvation experience to their lives (cf. Giles Conwill, "Black Preaching and Catholicism," *Ministry among Black Americans* [Indianapolis: Lilly Endowments, Inc., 1980], pp. 31–43).

Plenty Good Room, 99

Other Sources

When the lector has finished, the president addresses us and exhorts us to imitate the splendid things we have heard.

Justin Martyr

The same grace is needed for those who pronounce the prophecy as for those who hear it. And no one can understand the prophecy if the Spirit who prophesied does not grant him the understanding of his words.

Gregory the Great

Homilists are not there to make a presentation. They are there to engage a living people.

Kenneth Untener

One never preaches unless one has something to say.

Aidan Kavanagh

Background and Commentary

The homily springs from the scriptural readings for the celebration. Its intent is to interpret the word of God for our every-day lives, and to propose a challenge and direction for our lives as believers. This is not a sermon, neither is it scripture class, nor a time for deep exegesis or for didactic moral exhortation. The homily is to "break open" the scriptures, to proclaim the saving activity of God throughout history and in our world today. Usually the homily is given by the presiding priest or the deacon, but lay persons can preach in approved circumstances.

Profession of Faith

Scripture

I believe; help my unbelief!

Mark 9:24b

Jesus heard that they had driven [the man who had been born blind] out, and when he found him, he said, "Do you believe in the Son of Man?" He answered, "And who is he, sir? Tell me, so that I may believe in him." Jesus said to him, "You have seen him, and the one speaking with you is he." He said, "Lord, I believe."

John 9:35 – 37

If you confess with your lips that Jesus is Lord and believe in your heart that God raised him from the dead, you will be saved.

Romans 10:9

One Lord, one faith, one baptism, one God and Father of all, who is above all and through all and in all.

Ephesians 4:5 – 6

There is one God, the Father, from whom are all things and for whom we exist, and one Lord, Jesus Christ, through whom are all things and through whom we exist.

1 Corinthians 8:6

He was revealed in flesh, vindicated in spirit, seen by angels, proclaimed among Gentiles, believed in throughout the world, taken up in glory.

1 Timothy 3:16

Let the believer who is lowly boast in being raised up.

James 1:9

Documentation

The symbol or profession of faith in the celebration of Mass serves as a way for the people to respond and to give their assent to the word of God.

***General Instruction of the Roman Missal,* 43**

If it is sung, as a rule all are to sing it together or in alternation.

***General Instruction of the Roman Missal,* 44**

If the profession of faith occurs at the end of the liturgy of the word, the Apostles' Creed may be used with children, especially because it is part of their catechetical formation.

***Directory for Masses with Children,* 49**

It is usually preferable that the Creed be spoken in declamatory fashion rather than sung (NCCB, Nov. 1967). If it is sung, it might more effectively take the form of a simple musical declamation rather than an extensive and involved musical structure.

***Music in Catholic Worship,* 69**

The symbol, creed or profession of faith . . . has as its purpose in the celebration of Mass that the assembled congregation may respond and give assent to the word of God heard in the readings and through the homily.

***Lectionary for Mass: Introduction,* 29**

Other Sources

This is our faith, this is the faith of the Church.
We are proud to profess it in Christ Jesus the Lord.

Roman Rite

Blest are they who suffer in faith,
the glory of God is theirs.

David Haas

We walk by faith and not by sight;
no gracious words we hear
of him who spoke as none e'er spoke,
but we believe him near.
We may not touch his hands and side,
nor follow where he trod;
Yet in his promise we rejoice,
and cry "My Lord and God!"

Help then, O Lord, our unbelief,
and may our faith abound;
to call on you when you are near,
and seek where you are found:
That when our live of faith is done
in realms of clearer light
we may behold you as you are
in full and endless sight.

Henry Alford

He is of the house of David,
he is son of Mary.
truly he was born,
he ate and he drank.

Truly he was persecuted under Pontius Pilate,
truly he was crucified,
in the presence of heaven, earth, and hell.
Truly he was raised from the dead.

Ignatius of Antioch

Background and Commentary

The origin of the word *creed* is the Latin *credo,* which means "I believe." "Jesus is Lord" is one of the first credal formulas in the New Testament. The questions of the baptismal liturgy (Do you believe in God the Father . . . in Jesus Christ . . . in the Holy Spirit?) are the roots of the Apostles' Creed. The Nicene Creed is a more refined theological text; its original form came from the First Council of Nicaea in the year 325. That council was called to counter the heresy known as Arianism, which taught that Jesus was not truly God.

The Creed was not originally part of the eucharistic celebration. It was introduced into the liturgy as a safeguard against heresy, and to keep the Arians from receiving communion. Although Arianism died out, the recitation of the Creed during Mass remained.

Some liturgists recommend that the profession of faith be omitted except during the season of Easter and at celebrations of baptism; some recommend that the "question and answer" formula prescribed for the celebration of the Easter Vigil be used. Choral recitation of the profession of faith often falls flat in delivery and experience; pastoral practice suggests that perhaps the profession of faith need not be used as frequently as it is.

The profession of faith may be sung, although this need not be done frequently. This would be especially effective during the initiation liturgy at the Easter Vigil, and also at the presentation of the creed celebrated as part of Christian initiation. If this is done, the assembly should sing all or at least most of the text.

Another way to expand or embody the profession of faith is to employ a hymn or song. This comes from Protestant practice, where there is often a "hymn of the day," a sung text that echoes the gospel message of the day. This can be a wonderful way for the assembly to offer a statement of faith and a response to the word. The hymnals *RitualSong* and *Worship* (both published by GIA) provide in their indices lists of hymns appropriate for each Sunday of the liturgical year.

General Intercessions

Scripture

Answer when I call, faithful God,
You cleared away my trouble;
be good to me, listen to my prayer.

Psalm 4:2

Lord, hear the longing of the poor,
listen to their every word,
and give them heart.

Psalm 10:17

Praise is yours, God in Zion.
Now is the moment
to keep our vow,
for you, God, are listening.

You give victory
in answer to our prayer.

Psalm 65:2 – 3, 6a

God, do not be deaf,
do not be still,
do not be mute.

Psalm 83:2

I am filled with love,
for the Lord hears me;
the Lord bends to my voice
whenever I call.

Psalm 116:1– 2

Then Jesus told them a parable about their need to pray always and not to lose heart.

Luke 18:1

So I say to you, Ask, and it will be given you; search, and you will find; knock, and the door will be opened for you. For everyone who asks receives, and everyone who searches finds, and for everyone who knocks, the door will be opened.

Luke 11:9 –10

Do not worry about anything, but in everything by prayer and supplication with thanksgiving let your requests be made known to God.

Philippians 4:6

First of all, then, I urge that supplications, prayers, intercessions, and thanksgivings be made for everyone, for kings and all who are in high positions, so that we may lead a quiet and peaceable life in all godliness and dignity.

1 Timothy 2:1–2

Documentation

Especially on Sundays and holy days of obligation there is to be restored, after the gospel and the homily, "the universal prayer" or "the prayer of the faithful." By this prayer, in which the people are to take part, intercession shall be made for holy Church, for the civil authorities, for those oppressed by various needs, for all people, and for the salvation of the entire world.

Constitution on the Sacred Liturgy, 53

In the general intercessions or prayer of the faithful, the people, exercising their priestly function, intercede for all humanity.

General Instruction of the Roman Missal, 45

As a rule the sequence of intentions is:

a) for the needs of the Church;
b) for public authorities and the salvation of the world;
c) for those oppressed by any need;
d) for the local community.

In particular celebrations, such as confirmations, marriages, funerals, etc., the series of intercessions may refer more specifically to the occasion.

General Instruction of the Roman Missal, 46

It belongs to the priest celebrant to direct the general intercessions, by means of a brief introduction to invite the congregation to pray, and after the intercessions to say the concluding prayer. It is desirable that a deacon, cantor, or other person announce the intentions. The whole assembly gives expression to its supplication either by a response said together after each intention or by a silent prayer.

General Instruction of the Roman Missal, 47

Litanies are often more effective when sung. The repetition of melody and rhythm draws the people together in a strong and unified response. . . . The general intercessions (prayer of the faithful) offer an opportunity for litanical singing.

Music in Catholic Worship, 74

Enlightened by God's word and in a sense responding to it, the assembly of the faithful prays in the general intercessions as a rule for the needs of the universal church and the local community, for the salvation of the world and those oppressed by any burden, and for special categories of people.

Lectionary for Mass: Introduction, 30

Other Sources

If you believe and I believe and we together pray,
the Holy Spirit must come down and set God's people free.

Zimbabwean traditional

The form of the prayer of the faithful is not that of an acclamation, nor a response. It is a prayer in litany form.

Patrick Collins

Have you ever been annoyed when the prayer of the faithful is thrown open to personal petitions from the congregation? Your annoyance is legitimate. Often the private petitions can't be heard by the assembly, and too often people will use their petition as a platform for preaching about something.

Tad Guzie

Background and Commentary

The intercessions, like many other parts of the Mass, have roots in the Jewish synagogue service, which includes prayers of petition. It was not long after Christians began to gather on the Lord's day that this prayer became an integral part of the eucharistic celebration. History tells us that the intercessions had disappeared from the Roman rite before the reforms of the Second Vatican Council. The general intercessions are also known as the "prayer of the faithful," since in the early church, the intercessions took place after the catechumens were dismissed from the gathering.

The placement of the intercessions at the conclusion of the word service is logical: We have heard and dwelled on God's word, and we respond by and through our prayer for the church and the world.

The general intercessions as they are customarily prayed form one of the most impoverished moments of the liturgy. First of all, we lack a solid understanding of the purpose of the intercessions. Second, in light of this lack of understanding, the texts we compose are very poor and inappropriate. Third, the recitation of the intentions and the response does not embody the awareness and energy these prayers deserve.

Our approach to the general intercessions tends to be entangled in the individualistic and consumerist tendencies of our culture. We need to remember that in these prayers, we are not telling God what we think should be done for us, but rather, we are placing before God our needs and asking God to act as God wills, not as we will. To avoid this, I recommend that we eliminate the "that they" clause from our intercessions. When we approach these prayers in this mode, we are directing God toward our intended outcome, not God's. We do not pray for the sick "that they" may be healed or delivered on our schedule and on our terms, but we pray "for" them, that God may be attentive and present to them.

We often forget that these prayers are petitionary in nature, not prayers of thanksgiving. We intercede with God for the needs of creation. At Mass, our prayer of thanks for what God has done is the eucharistic prayer.

Many parishes have too many intercessions, and each one is verbose. Writing good intercessions is a skill; intercessions require careful crafting and editing. The *General Instruction* gives us clear guidelines as to the intent and content of the prayers. Ordinarily, the prayers are directed (1) for the church; (2) for the world and its leaders; (3) for those who suffer from injustice and oppression; and (4) for the needs of the local community. This general pattern should be the basis for the composition of the general intercessions. The prayers are usually introduced by the presider, and the deacon or one of the readers announces the petitions. The petitions may also be intoned by the cantor. While the assembly's response is usually "Lord, hear our prayer," other texts may be used as long as the character of the response does not change.

Musicians should give consideration to the intercessions as sung prayer. Musical presentation of the intercessions gives them more weight liturgically; it elevates them to a position of true intercession and prayer, rather than a list of requests. In addition, a musical presentation of the prayers helps bring the liturgy of the word to a satisfying conclusion.

There are many settings of the prayers of the faithful by many composers and publishers, and good tones to which the intercessions may be sung. They could be sung in a litanic style, with the petitions sung by the cantor followed by a common response by the assembly; or the assembly could sing an ostinato, a mantra-like refrain, over and over again. The cantor then sings (or the reader recites) the individual petitions over the refrain. This requires a certain amount of creativity and practice. But no matter what format is chosen, musical presentation of the general intercessions can lead to a renewed appreciation and prayerful experience of these prayers.

Notes

chapter THREE

The Liturgy of the Eucharist

General Background

Scripture

Day by day, as they spent much time together in the temple, they broke bread at home and ate their food with glad and generous hearts, praising God and having the goodwill of all the people.

Acts 2:46 – 47

Documentation

At the last supper Christ instituted the sacrifice and paschal meal that make the sacrifice of the cross to be continually present in the Church.

General Instruction of the Roman Missal, 48

Other Sources

And we accept bread at his table,
Broken and shared, a living sign.
Here in this world, dying and living,
We are each other's bread and wine.
This is the place where we can receive
What we need to increase:
God's justice and God's peace.

Huub Oosterhuis

Background and Commentary

We look to our Jewish roots once again to understand our liturgy. The Last Supper was probably a celebration of the Passover meal (though we do not know this for certain), the ritual dinner at which the Jewish people's redemption from slavery is remembered and rejoiced over. This event gives us the structure of the liturgy of the eucharist: taking bread, offering a blessing prayer over the bread and wine, breaking the bread, and sharing the bread and wine. These actions are the primary elements of this ritual. Throughout history, the liturgy of the eucharist has gone through many changes, adaptations and developments, but for the most part the basic structure has remained consistent. The reforms of the Second Vatican Council sought to simplify the liturgy of the eucharist; it now comprises the following elements:

Preparation of the Table and Gifts with song
Eucharistic Prayer
- Preface
- Holy, Holy
- Epiclesis
- Institution Narrative
- Memorial Acclamation
- Anamnesis
- Offering
- Intercessions
- Concluding Doxology
- Great Amen

Communion Rite
- The Lord's Prayer
- The Sign of Peace
- Breaking of the Bread and Lamb of God
- Invitation to Communion
- Communion Procession
- Silent Prayer and Song of Praise
- Prayer after Communion

Because of history and devotional faith, many people participate in this part of the Mass individually and inwardly, rather than as part of a community. This is important for music ministers to understand. Music creatively and thoughtfully put to use can lead people out of this privatistic way of experiencing the liturgy of the eucharist. The entire liturgy of the eucharist has a musical and lyrical quality. The challenge for music ministers is not to insert musical "station breaks" into this part of the Mass, but to help reveal the unity of it. The assembly can then experience it is as a satisfying and complete prayerful journey, not just a series of separate liturgical snippets.

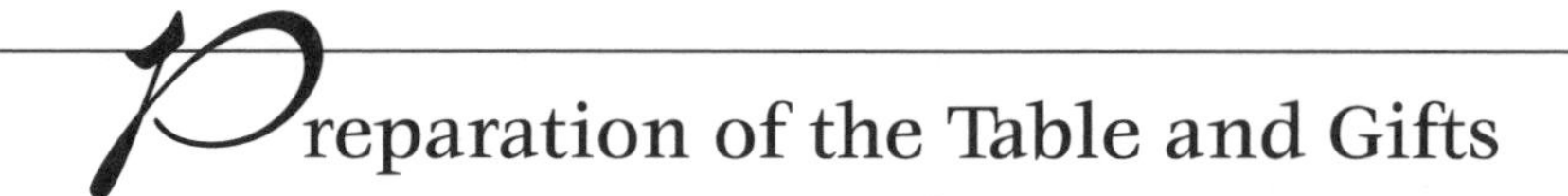

Preparation of the Table and Gifts

Scripture

No one shall appear before me empty-handed. The choicest of the first fruits of your ground you shall bring into the house of the Lord your God.

Exodus 23:15, 19

You spread a table before me
as my foes look on.

Psalm 23:5a

I wash my hands in innocence
and walk around your altar,
singing a song of thanks,
telling your wonderful deeds.

Psalm 26:6 –7

Documentation

It is desirable for the faithful to present the bread and wine, which are accepted by the priest or deacon at a convenient place. . . . Even though the faithful no longer . . . bring the bread and wine from their homes, the rite of carrying up the gifts retains the same spiritual value and meaning. This is also the time to receive money or other gifts for the church or the poor.

General Instruction of the Roman Missal, 49

It is fitting that the faithful's participation be expressed by their presenting both the bread and wine for the celebration of the eucharist and other gifts for the needs of the church and of the poor.

General Instruction of the Roman Missal, 101

The procession can be accompanied by song. Song is not always necessary or desirable. Organ or instrumental music is also fitting at this time. . . . The song need not speak of bread and wine or of offering. The proper function of this song is to accompany and celebrate the communal aspects of the procession. The text, therefore, can be any appropriate song of praise or of rejoicing in keeping with the season.

The Place of Music in Eucharistic Celebration

The eucharistic prayer is preceded by the preparation of the gifts. The purpose of this rite is to prepare bread and wine for the sacrifice. The secondary character of the rite determines the manner of celebration. It consists very simply of bringing the gifts to the altar, possibly accompanied by song, prayers to be said by the celebrant as he prepares the gifts, and the prayer over the gifts. Of these elements the bringing of the gifts, the placing of the gifts on the altar, and the prayer over the gifts are primary. All else is secondary.

Music in Catholic Worship, 46

Song may accompany the procession and preparation of the gifts. It is not always necessary or desirable. Organ or instrumental music is also fitting at the time. When song is used, it need not speak of bread and wine or of offering. The proper function of this song is to accompany and celebrate the communal aspects of the procession. The text, therefore, can be any appropriate song of praise or of rejoicing in keeping with the season. . . . Instrumental interludes can effectively accompany the procession and preparation of the gifts and thus keep this part of the Mass in proper perspective relative to the eucharistic prayer which follows.

Music in Catholic Worship, 71

The proper place of silence must not be neglected, and the temptation must be resisted to cover every moment with music (GIRM, 23; GILOTH, 202; Paul VI, Apostolic Exhortation, *Evangelica Testificatio* [29 June, 1971], 46). There are times when an instrumental interlude is able to bridge the gap between two parts of a ceremony and help to unify the liturgical action. But music's function is always ministerial and must never degenerate into idle background music.

Liturgical Music Today, 59

The Order of Mass sets up an order of preference: a) the priest says the formulas in a low voice *(secreto)* during the singing; b) if there is no singing or music, the priest says the texts quietly; or he *may (licet)* c) say them aloud; d) *if* there is no song and *if* the priest says the formulas aloud, the people *may (potest)* say the acclamations at the end (cf. Order of Mass, nos. 91, 21).

Bishops' Committee on the Liturgy Newsletter

Other Sources

The table which you set has the riches of the fields;
How wondrous are your gifts to us.
You share the finest portion, Lord,
with rev'rence and with grace;
How wondrous are your gifts to us.
Abundant is your love;
How wondrous are your gifts to us.

Michael Balhoff, Gary Daigle, Darryl Ducote

We place upon your table a gleaming cloth of white:
the weaving of our stories, the fabric of our lives;
the dreams of those before us, the ancient hopeful cries,
the promise of our future:
our needing and our nurture lie here before our eyes.

We place upon your table a humble loaf of bread:
the gift of field and hillside, the grain by which we're fed;
we come to taste the presence of him on whom we feed,
to strength and connect us,
to challenge and correct us, to love in word and deed.

We place upon your table a simple cup of wine:
the fruit of human labor, the gift of sun and vine;
we come to taste the presence of him we claim as Lord,
his dying and his living,
his leading and his giving, his love in cup outpoured.

We gather 'round your table, we pause within our quest,
we stand beside our neighbors, we name the stranger "guest."
The feast is spread before us; you bid us come and dine;
in blessing we'll uncover,
in sharing we'll discover your substance and your sign.

We come to your feast,
we come to your feast,
the young and old,
the frightened, the bold,
the greatest and the least.
We come to your feast,
we come to your feast
with the fruit of our lands
and the work of our hands,
we come to your feast.

Michael Joncas

Now the silence, Now the peace,
Now the empty hands uplifted;
Now the kneeling, Now the plea,
Now the Father's arms in welcome;
Now the hearing, Now the pow'r,
Now the vessel brimmed for pouring;
Now the body, Now the blood,
Now the joyful celebration;
Now the wedding, Now the songs,
Now the heart forgiven leaping;
Now the Spirit's visitation,
Now the Son's epiphany,
Now the Father's blessing.
Now. Now. Now.

Jaroslav J. Vajda

Then bread and a cup of wine mixed with water are brought to him who presides.

Justin Martyr

You are blessed, Lord our God,
King of the universe,
you who created the fruit of the vine.

You are blessed, Lord our God,
King of the universe,
you who have brought bread forth from the earth.

The *Kiddush*

Background and Commentary

The word "offertory" is often used for this part of the Mass, but this is incorrect. Nothing is being offered at this moment. This is a preparatory time; thus the name "Preparation of the Gifts." What happens during this time is primarily functional. We collect the gifts of money for the poor and for the church, and we bring them forward; we bring the gifts of bread and wine forward and we prepare them.

Bread, wine and the collection, symbols of the community, are the gifts to be brought forward. Other objects should not be brought forward. Other items that will be needed for the preparation (water, corporal, purificator, cup and sacramentary) should be brought from a side table. When there is music, which is most of the time, the presider silently prays the prayers over the bread and wine (Blessed are you, Lord, God of all creation . . .); when there is no music, the presider may speak the prayers aloud, and the assembly may respond. The prayers that accompany the commingling of water and wine and the washing of hands are prayed quietly by the presider.

At the conclusion of the preparation, the presider invites the assembly to pray that God accept the gifts.

This functional, preparatory time should not be rushed, but it does not call for much ritual weight or elaboration. Some liturgists describe this moment as a sort of intermission between the liturgy of the word and the liturgy of the eucharist. The analogy need not be taken literally, but this rite is less important than the primary rites.

The liturgical documents are very helpful to musicians regarding this rite. The texts of music chosen for the preparation should not focus on bread and wine. A seasonal motif or a song of praise is more appropriate. Congregational music is fine, but the documents direct — and pastoral practice affirms — that we use other approaches for the preparatory rite. Instrumental music or a selection by the choir or schola alone works very well, especially when it is timed to accompany the action. Neither by length nor by emotional power should the music overshadow the rite or draw too much attention to itself.

Silence is an option to consider, although, like any music, there are times when it is appropriate and times when it is not.

Eucharistic Prayer

Scripture

When he was at table with them, he took bread, blessed and broke it, and gave it to them. Then their eyes were opened, and they recognized him.

Luke 24:30 – 31a

On the first day of the week, when we met to break bread, Paul was holding a discussion with them; since he intended to leave the next day, he continued speaking until midnight. Then Paul went upstairs, and after he had broken bread and eaten, he continued to converse with them until dawn.

Acts 20:7– 8, 11a

Documentation

Now the center and summit of the whole celebration begins: the eucharistic prayer, a prayer of thanksgiving and sanctification. The priest invites the people to lift up their hearts to the Lord in prayer and thanks; he unites them with himself in the prayer he addresses in their name to the Father through Jesus Christ. The meaning of the prayer is that the entire congregation joins itself to Christ in acknowledging the great things God has done and in offering the sacrifice.

General Instruction of the Roman Missal, 54

The eucharistic prayer calls for all to listen in silent reverence, but also to take part through the acclamations.

General Instruction of the Roman Missal, 55

As a statement of the faith of the local assembly it is affirmed and ratified by all those present through acclamations of faith: the first acclamation or Sanctus, the memorial acclamation, and the Great Amen.

Music in Catholic Worship, 47

The acclamations are shouts of joy which arise from the whole assembly as forceful and meaningful assents to God's Word and Action. They are important because they make some of the most significant moments of the Mass . . . stand out. It is of their nature that they be rhythmically strong, melodically appealing, and affirmative. The people should know the acclamations by heart in order to sing them spontaneously. Some variety is recommended and even imperative. The challenge to the composer and people alike is one of variety without confusion.

Music in Catholic Worship, 53

The acclamations (. . . including the special acclamations of praise in the Eucharistic Prayers of Masses with Children) are the preeminent sung prayers of the eucharistic liturgy. Singing these acclamations makes their prayer all the more effective.

Liturgical Music Today, 17

Other Sources

You are blessed, Lord our God,
King of the universe,
you who nourish the entire world
with goodness, tender love, and mercy.
you are blessed, O Lord,
you who nourish the universe.

We will give you thanks, Lord our God,
for you have given us a desirable land for our inheritance,
[that we may eat of its fruits
and be filled with its goodness].
You are blessed, Lord our God,
for the land and the food.

Lord our God, take pity
on Israel your people and Jerusalem your city,
on Zion, the place where your glory dwells,
on your altar and your sanctuary.
You are blessed, O Lord, who build Jerusalem.
You are blessed, Lord our God,
King of the universe,
(you who are) good and filled with kindness!

Birkat ha-mazon

The heart of the prayer is praise.

Thomas Porter

We need to know the difference between mood music and music that engages.

Edward Foley

We need to experience a eucharistic prayer that says, yes, we are the holy people of God and glad to be, but the price of it is death, death even unto the cross.

Ralph Keifer

Ownership and participation, both silent and sung, are the nature of the prayer.

Mary McGann

Occasional acclamations, however lofty, do not conquer the deadening effect of long periods of spoken text. The desire often voiced to have even more acclamations only names the disease; it does not offer the needed solution.

Peter Fink

I believe that Jesus was a singer.

Robert Haas

Background and Commentary

The eucharistic prayer has its roots in Jewish worship. Its structure is much like that of a particular form of Jewish blessing prayer, the *berakah.* The *berakah* was and is used by Jews for both private prayer and communal gatherings. In shorter forms, Jews use it to bless God for the many gifts we encounter throughout the day. Longer forms are used at more formal moments; including prayers of thanks and praise over bread and wine.

As the Christian church developed, the *berakah* was adapted to the needs of the new movement. In early times, the bishop would improvise the eucharistic prayer according to its structure. Later, the prayer became more regulated. These established prayers took on various forms in the East and in the West. They were sometimes known as canons, which indicated they were the established prayer of the liturgy. Now we use the term "eucharistic prayer," focusing on the prayer as thanksgiving. The prayer is a remembrance and celebration of the great works of God throughout time, of God's activity in our lives here and now, and of God's reign here and to come. The prayer can be seen as a summary of our Christian life centered in the eucharist.

Current Eucharistic Prayers For many generations, there was one prescribed eucharistic prayer in the Roman Catholic church, the Roman Canon, now known as Eucharistic Prayer I. As a result of the liturgical reforms of the Second Vatican Council, more eucharistic prayers have been composed or adapted from earlier prayers.

Eucharistic Prayer I may be used any time. It finds a particular home at the proper celebrations of Christmas, Epiphany, Holy Thursday, certain times during the Easter season and at Pentecost.

Eucharistic Prayer II is an adaptation of a prayer in an ancient Christian text, the *Apostolic Tradition,* which is believed to have been written by Hippolytus of Rome in the early third century. It has its own preface, but others may be used. It is the shortest of the newer prayers.

Eucharistic Prayer III is a modern composition with sources in many prayers of the Eastern and Western church. It may be used with any of the prefaces in the sacramentary.

Eucharistic Prayer IV is highly theological and scriptural, and is the longest of the newer prayers. It is adapted from a eucharistic prayer that is still used in the Eastern church. It has its own preface, which must be used with it.

In addition to the four core eucharistic prayers, there are other eucharistic prayers which are to be used at certain times. The three Eucharistic Prayers for Masses with Children are for use when large numbers of children are present. What sets them apart is the language, which is intended to be accessible to children, and the more frequent and flexible acclamations sung by the assembly. The second of these three prayers has more acclamations than any other: the assembly sings twelve acclamations in this prayer.

The two Eucharistic Prayers for Masses of Reconciliation are especially appropriate during the season of Lent. The Eucharistic Prayers for Masses for Various Occasions (really one prayer with several prefaces) may be used for particular intentions or events.

Prayer of the Entire Assembly

> Now the center and summit of the entire celebration begins: the eucharistic prayer, a prayer of thanksgiving and sanctification. The priest invites the people to lift up their hearts to the Lord in prayer and thanks; he unites them with himself in the prayer he addresses *in their name* to the Father through Jesus Christ. The meaning of the prayer is that the *entire congregation joins itself to Christ* in acknowledging the great things God has done and in offering the sacrifice. (*General Instruction of the Roman Missal,* 54, emphasis added)

In other words, the assembly prays the prayer together, in unity as the Body of Christ. The eucharistic prayer is not the private prayer of the priest. We together with the priest call upon God in giving thanks, in calling the Spirit to be present, in the celebration of the gifts of bread and wine; and in the actions of remembrance, offering, intercession and praise.

Unfortunately, quite often, the experience is that it is the priest's prayer. This is partly because the prayer is structured largely as a monologue, and the priest's voice and presence are dominant throughout. Missalettes, hymnals and other worship aids make it easy for the members of the assembly to follow along passively in their printed copies of the prayer. When people are merely reading along with the priest, they are not engaged as equal partners in the prayer.

The eucharistic prayer is primarily a prayer of thanksgiving, not one of petition or penitence. Consider this section of Eucharistic Prayer II: "We thank you for counting us worthy to stand in your presence and serve you." As we pray in these words, what posture are we in? On our knees! The official directives for the liturgy in the United States call for the assembly to assume a posture of penitence, even as the text being proclaimed calls the assembly to stand and give thanks for being worthy to serve. This sense of worthiness is further obscured when, before we receive communion, we pray (on our knees), "Lord, I am not worthy." Issues like these ensure that discussions among liturgical scholars, practitioners and church authorities will continue for ages to come — as it should be.

Music and the Eucharistic Prayer In the meantime, attention and creativity will help the assembly to pray and experience the eucharistic prayer as a unity, as the prayer of the church. Music ministers have not paid enough attention to the musical nature of the prayer, or to its need for strong, effective and durable acclamations.

We tend to change the acclamations in the eucharistic prayer far too often. Repetition is an important principle in ritual music. The three primary acclamations of the prayer (Holy, Holy, memorial acclamation, and Great Amen) need to be known well by the assembly; they need to be sung by heart. The only way to achieve that is repetition. A setting of the acclamations that can stand the needed amount of repetition without losing its freshness and vitality is a setting that is worthy of the assembly's prayer.

Second, the eucharistic acclamations need to have a unity of their own. They are generally composed as a unit; we should honor that. Do not choose for one celebration settings of these three acclamations that come from different musical compositions or styles. The unity of the prayer will be more evident when the musical elements are unified.

The eucharistic prayer achieves the greatest unity when the entire prayer is musical, when the presider sings the prayer in dialogue with the people. Thus the acclamations truly flow from the proclamations that precede them. Marty Haugen's "Mass of Creation" (GIA) led the way for many composers, liturgists and music ministers to see the eucharistic prayer as a lyrical and musical event. A unified composition and rendition makes the unity of the prayer evident. Not every parish priest can sing, but more priests could sing the prayer than do now, especially if parish musicians help.

Finally, the acclamations used need to be truly acclamatory; they must also be given primary musical weight in terms of presentation and arrangement. How often have we experienced a liturgy where the opening and closing songs are elaborate, with arrangements for SATB choir, brass, percussion and organ, but the acclamations have minimal arrangements, and no energy or excitement. We need to reverse our musical energies and priorities – these acclamations need to be given our best, in presentation and passion.

The liturgical and pastoral demands of the Eucharistic Prayer are many, but our primary concern should be how this prayer can be experienced as fully as possible, as the prayer and praise of the entire worshiping community.

Preface

Scripture

You alone are holy.
What god compares to you?
You are the God of power,
strong among the nations.
You reached out to save your people,
the children of Jacob and Joseph.

Psalm 77:14–16

The Lord be with your spirit. Grace be with you.

2 Timothy 4:22

Documentation

Thanksgiving (expressed especially in the preface): in the name of the entire people of God, the priest praises the Father and gives thanks to him for the whole work of salvation or for some special aspect of it that corresponds with the day, feast, or season.

General Instruction of the Roman Missal, 55a

By an introductory dialogue the priest invites the people to lift their hearts to God in praise and thanks.

Music in Catholic Worship, 47

Other Sources

He is to say the thanksgiving:
The Lord be with you!
And with your spirit!
Let us lift up our hearts.
They are turned to the Lord.
Let us give thanks to the Lord!
It is right and just!

Apostolic Tradition

Background and Commentary

The preface is a proclamation, not a foreword. It begins with the dialogue, which makes a strong statement that the presider is in partnership with the assembly in the praying of this great prayer. Following the ancient Jewish pattern of this prayer, the presider, in the name of the entire assembly, offers praise to God for the gifts of creation and for God's presence in our lives. Prefaces vary according to the season or feast being celebrated. There are many options in the sacramentary for the preface.

The preface is most effective when sung. Singing heightens the proclamation of the prayer; it also leads into the assembly's singing of the Holy, Holy.

Holy, Holy

Scripture

And one called to another and said: "Holy, holy, holy is the LORD of hosts; the whole earth is full of his glory." The pivots on the thresholds shook at the voices of those who called, and the house filled with smoke.

Isaiah 6:34

And the Word became flesh and lived among us, and we have seen his glory.

John 1:14

Blest is the one who comes,
who comes in the name of the Lord.

Psalm 118:26

The crowds that went ahead of him and that followed were shouting, "Hosanna to the Son of David! Blessed is the one who comes in the name of the Lord! Hosanna in the highest heaven!"

Matthew 21:9

Then those who went ahead and those who followed were shouting, "Blessed is the one who comes in the name of Lord! Blessed is the coming kingdom of our ancestor David! Hosanna in the highest heaven!"

Mark 11:9–10

Blessed is the king who comes in the name of the Lord!

Luke 19:38a

Day and night without ceasing they sing, "Holy, holy, holy, the Lord God the almighty, who was and is and is to come."

Revelation 4:8b

Documentation

Acclamation: joining with the angels, the congregation sings . . . the Sanctus. This acclamation is an intrinsic part of the eucharistic prayer, and all the people join with the priest in singing . . . it.

***General Instruction of the Roman Missal,* 55b**

This is the people's acclamation of praise concluding the preface of the eucharistic prayer. We join the whole communion of saints in acclaiming the Lord. Settings which add harmony or descants on solemn feasts and occasions are appropriate, but since this chant belongs to priest and people, the choir parts must facilitate and make effective the people's parts.

***Music in Catholic Worship,* 56**

Other Sources

Let God be the object of our pride and confidence. Let us submit to his will. Let us contemplate the entire multitude of his angels and consider how they stand ready and serve his will. . . . We too, then, should assemble in oneness of mind and cry out to him perseveringly, as with a single mouth, that we might share in his great and glorious promises.

Clement of Rome

We also make mention of the Seraphim, whom Isaiah contemplated when he was caught up in an ecstasy by the Holy Spirit. They encircled the throne of God. They had two wings to hide their faces, two wings to cover their feet, and two wings for flying. And they were exclaiming, "Holy, holy, holy is the Lord Sabaoth!" We sing this doxology, which comes to us from the Seraphim, in order that we may participate in the song of the heavenly armies.

Cyril of Jerusalem

This acclamation . . . needs to be recognized as integral to the prayer, and not as an interruption.

Peter Fink

Background and Commentary

This text is among the earliest of eucharistic prayers. It is inspired by Isaiah's vision of heaven (Isaiah 6:3 – 4). Its invocation of the heavenly angels makes it a logical conclusion to the preface prayer. The last part of this text, "Blessed is he who comes . . ." was part of the crowd's acclamation of Christ on Passion Sunday. It was joined to the Sanctus text early in the church's tradition.

This acclamation is to be sung by all, completely. Any choral or instrumental embellishment (which by no means is to be discouraged) should never overpower the assembly or cause them to be timid in their own singing. It is best when a community knows one or two settings of this acclamation, just as for all the other acclamations, well enough to sing it by heart. This acclamation follows the preface prayer. It is effective for an instrumentalist (pianist, organist, guitarist) to begin playing quietly behind the concluding words of the preface so that the acclamation can blossom forth at the right time.

Epiclesis

Scripture

You created all of them
by your Spirit,
and you give new life
to the earth.

Psalm 104:30

God is spirit, and those who worship him must worship in spirit and truth.

John 4:24

Pray in the Spirit at all times in every prayer and supplication.

Ephesians 6:18a

Do not quench the Spirit.

1 Thessalonians 5:19

Documentation

Epiclesis: in special invocations the Church calls on God's power and asks that the gifts offered . . . be consecrated, that is, become Christ's body and blood.

***General Instruction of the Roman Missal,* 54c**

Other Sources

We ask God, the lover of mankind, to send the Holy Spirit on the offerings that are set forth there, in order that he may change the bread into the body of Christ and the wine into the blood of Christ. For whatever the Spirit touches is sanctified and transformed.

Cyril of Jerusalem

Background and Commentary

Epiclesis comes from a Greek word that means "invocation." In this context, it refers to the invoking of the Holy Spirit upon the gifts of bread and wine to transform these elements as well as the assembly who has come together. The epiclesis in Eucharistic Prayer I does not explicitly mention the Holy Spirit ("Bless and approve our offering . . ."). The Eastern churches tend to put more emphasis on the epiclesis than the Roman church does. The Roman rite gives more emphasis to the institution narrative.

Institution Narrative

Scripture

While they were eating, Jesus took a loaf of bread, and after blessing it he broke it, gave it to the disciples, and said, "Take, eat; this is my body." Then he took a cup, and after giving thanks he gave it to them, saying, "Drink from it, all of you; for this is my blood of the covenant, which is poured out for many for the forgiveness of sins. I tell you, I will never again drink of this fruit of the vine until that day when I drink it new with you in my Father's kingdom."

Matthew 26:26 – 29

While they were eating, he took a loaf of bread, and after blessing it he broke it, gave it to them, and said, "Take; this is my body." Then he took a cup, and after giving thanks he gave it to them, and all of them drank from it. He said to them, "This is my blood of the covenant, which is poured out for many. Truly I tell you, I will never again drink of the fruit of the vine until that day when I drink it new in the kingdom of God."

Mark 14:22 – 25

When the hour came, he took his place at the table, and the apostles with him. He said to them, "I have eagerly desired to eat this Passover with you before I suffer; for I tell you, I will not eat it until it is fulfilled in the kingdom of God." Then he took a cup, and after giving thanks he said, "Take this and divide it among yourselves; for I tell you that from now on I will not drink of the fruit of the vine until the kingdom of God comes." Then he took a loaf of bread, and when he had given thanks, he broke it and gave it to them, saying, "This is my body, which is given for you. Do this in remembrance of me." And he did the same with the cup after supper, saying, "This cup that is poured out for you is the new covenant in my blood."

Luke 22:14 – 20

For I received from the Lord what I also handed on to you, that the Lord Jesus on the night when he was betrayed took a loaf of bread, and when he had given thanks, he broke it and said, "This is my body that is for you. Do this in remembrance of me." In the same way he took the cup also, after supper, saying, "This cup is the new covenant in my blood. Do this, as often as you drink it, in remembrance of me." For as often as you eat this bread and drink the cup, you proclaim the Lord's death until he comes.

1 Corinthians 11:23 – 26

Documentation

Institution narrative and consecration: in the words and actions of Christ, that sacrifice is celebrated which he himself instituted at the Last Supper, when, under the appearances of bread and wine, he offered his body and blood, gave them to his apostles to eat and drink, then commanded that they carry on this mystery.

General Instruction of the Roman Missal, 54d

Background and Commentary

The institution narrative is the heart of the eucharistic prayer; it has been an integral part of the eucharistic prayer since the earliest days of the church. The Western church's emphasis on this narrative as the words of consecration has sometimes given it too much weight, thus unbalancing the prayer as a whole.

The four scriptural accounts of the institution of the eucharist at the Last Supper are the foundation of the narrative. Of these, Paul's account in 1 Corinthians is the earliest, preceding the descriptions in the three synoptic gospels by many years

The recounting of the institution of the eucharist is an important element of our celebration of the eucharist, but this does not mean that the Mass is to be a historical re-enactment of the Last Supper. Those who plan and celebrate the liturgy need to avoid anything that tends in that direction. Perhaps the most common example is when the presider breaks the eucharistic bread as he says, "he broke the bread." More egregious errors are sometimes seen on Holy Thursday — for instance, the Mass of the Lord's Supper celebrated with twelve men in costume around the priest. Such an approach is an obstacle to understanding the Mass as the act of this community in this time and this place. It must be avoided.

Ringing bells during the eucharistic prayer is a practice held over from the days when people did not understand what was going on in the Mass and had to be alerted to the "important parts." It is still permitted, but it reinforces the idea that the consecration is all that really matters, working against the unity of the prayer.

The presider may sing the institution narrative, but only if the entire prayer is sung, so that the balance of the entire prayer is maintained.

Memorial Acclamation

Scripture

For as often as you eat this bread and drink the cup, you proclaim the Lord's death until he comes.

1 Corinthians 11:26

Astounding mystery
at the heart of our faith:

One who appeared in human flesh, alleluia!
was attested by the Spirit, alleluia!
seen by angels, alleluia!
proclaimed to Gentiles, alleluia!
believed in by the world, alleluia!
taken up in glory, alleluia!

1 Timothy 3:16

Documentation

We support one another's faith in the paschal mystery, the central mystery of our belief. This acclamation is properly a memorial of the Lord's suffering and glorification, with an expression of faith in his coming. Variety in text and music is desirable.

Music in Catholic Worship, 57

Other Sources

We announce your death,
we proclaim your resurrection,
and we pray . . .

The Euchology of Der Balyzeh

Memorial acclamations ought to be expressions of the assembly's remembering.

Peter Fink

We remember how you loved us to your death,
and still we celebrate, for you are with us here.
And we believe that we will see you when you come
in your glory, Lord,
we remember, we celebrate, we believe.

Marty Haugen

Background and Commentary

The memorial acclamation is a recent element of the eucharistic prayer, having come into use with the Second Vatican Council. Recent it may be, but it is certainly theologically and pastorally sound. The priest or deacon invites the community to "proclaim the mystery of faith" and the community responds with one of four texts:

> Christ has died,
> Christ is risen,
> Christ will come again.
>
> Dying you destroyed our death,
> rising you restored our life,
> Lord Jesus, come in glory.
>
> When we eat this bread and drink this cup,
> we proclaim your death, Lord Jesus,
> until you come in glory.
>
> Lord, by your cross and resurrection
> you have set us free.
> You are the savior of the world.

The first of these seems to be the most popular; the text is very strong and direct. "Dying you destroyed our death" is addressed to Christ directly, and is especially appropriate for the season of Advent. Since the eucharistic bread and wine are shared by all, the third acclamation text, "When we eat this bread," is a good choice. The weakest of the options, "Lord, by your cross," is the only text that has no mention of Christ's coming again in glory.

The memorial acclamation is to be sung by the assembly in its entirety, and should be strong and compact. Musically, this can be difficult to accomplish; music ministers should choose the setting for this acclamation thoughtfully.

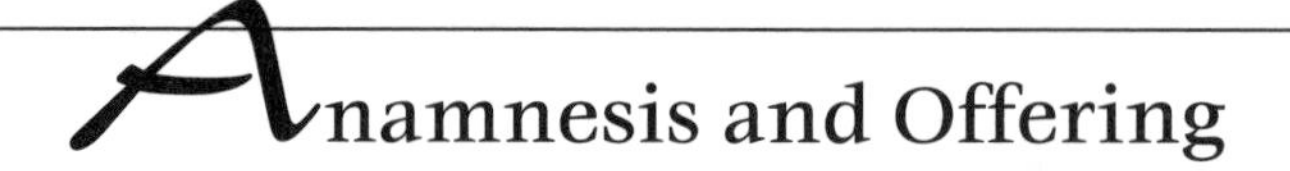

Anamnesis and Offering

Scripture

The Advocate, the Holy Spirit, whom the Father will send in my name, will teach you everything, and remind you of all that I have said to you.

John 14:26

When the Spirit of truth comes, he will guide you into all the truth. . . . He will declare to you the things that are to come.

John 16:13

Therefore be imitators of God, as beloved children, and live in love, as Christ loved us and gave himself up for us, a fragrant offering and sacrifice to God.

Ephesians 5:1–2

But even if I am being poured out as a libation over the sacrifice and the offering of your faith, I am glad and rejoice with all of you — and in the same way you also must be glad and rejoice with me.

Philippians 2:17–18

For by a single offering he has perfected for all time those who are sanctified.

Hebrews 10:14

Documentation

Anamnesis: in fulfillment of the command received from Christ through the apostles, the Church keeps his memorial by recalling especially his passion, resurrection, and ascension.

***General Instruction of the Roman Missal,* 55e**

Offering: in this memorial, the Church — and in particular the Church here and now assembled — offers the spotless victim to the Father in the Holy Spirit.

***General Instruction of the Roman Missal,* 55f**

Background and Commentary

Anamnesis means, in Greek, "to remember." To remember in this context is more than recalling the past redeeming deeds of Christ; it is to make them present among us now, and to hold them as a vision for the future. We do not remember for the sake of nostalgia; we remember to make that salvation and redemption present in our own lives. The salvation accomplished by Christ for us is a present, living reality.

The prayer of offering flows from the anamnesis. It is the remembering that allows us to make our offering Christ's, at this very gathering. This is why we hear the phrases referring to the sacrifice as "holy," "living," "acceptable" and "perfect." The bread is "life-giving," and the cup is "saving."

Intercessions

Scripture

Likewise the Spirit helps us in our weakness; for we do not know how to pray as we ought, but that very Spirit intercedes with sighs too deep for words. And God, who searches the heart, knows what is the mind of the Spirit, because the Spirit intercedes for the saints according to the will of God.

Romans 8:26 – 27

Documentation

Intercessions: the intercessions make it clear that the eucharist is celebrated in communion with the entire Church of heaven and earth and that the offering is made for the Church and all its members, living and dead, who are called to share in the salvation and redemption purchased by Christ's body and blood.

General Instruction of the Roman Missal, 55g

Other Sources

May your blessing come upon your people
who do your will.

Raise up the fallen,
bring back those who have strayed,
console the fainthearted.
For you are above every principality,
power, force, and dominion,
above everything that can be named
in this world and in the world to come.

The Euchology of Der Balyzeh

Good and gracious God, hear and remember us.

Marty Haugen

Background and Commentary

Intercession is an important genre of liturgical prayer, and has always been an integral part of Jewish meal prayer. The intercessory prayers invoke the saints, and ask God to look with favor upon the people gathered here and all who have died in God's friendship.

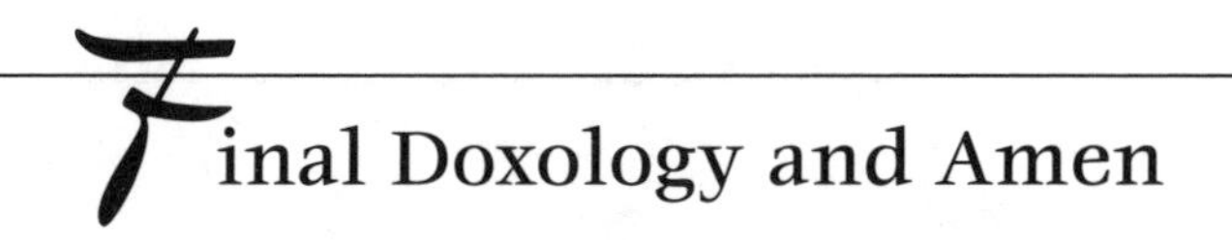

Final Doxology and Amen

Scripture

Let all the people sing
"Amen! Hallelujah!"

Psalm 106:48b

For from him and through him and to him are all things. To him be the glory forever. Amen.

Romans 11:36

For us there is one God, the Father, from whom are all things and for whom we exist, and one Lord, Jesus Christ, through whom are all things and through whom we exist.

1 Corinthians 8:6

For in him every one of God's promises is a "Yes." For this reason it is through him that we say the "Amen," to the glory of God.

2 Corinthians 1:20

For in him all things in heaven and on earth were created, things visible and invisible, whether thrones or dominions or rulers or powers — all things have been created through him and for him. He himself is before all things, and in him all things hold together.

Colossians 1:16–17

And the four living creatures said, "Amen!" And the elders fell down and worshiped.

Revelation 5:14

Documentation

Final doxology: the praise of God is expressed in the doxology, to which the people's acclamation is an assent and a conclusion.

***General Instruction of the Roman Missal,* 55h**

The worshipers assent to the eucharistic prayer and make it their own in the Great Amen. To be most effective, the Amen may be repeated or augmented. Choirs may harmonize and expand upon the people's acclamation.

***Music in Catholic Worship,* 58**

Other Sources

When the prayers and eucharist are finished, all the people present give their assent with an "Amen!" "Amen" in Hebrew means "So be it!"

Justin Martyr

In saying "Amen" to the justice of God proclaimed in the liturgy, we are by implication saying "Anathema" to all that fails to measure up to that justice.

Mark Searle

The end of the prayer should soar, not whimper.

Peter Fink

Be careful when you say "Amen."

Barbara Schmich

Background and Commentary

It is only appropriate that this great prayer conclude with a resounding "Amen," (which means "so be it") by the gathered assembly, just as the early Jewish meal prayers concluded with the same Amen. The doxology proclaimed — preferably sung — by the priest is a summary proclamation of the awe and wonder of the entire eucharist; the assembly is called upon to give its assent and affirmation as the bread and wine are held high.

Musically, this is the most important acclamation of the entire liturgy, and, of course, it is always sung. Even if the doxology is not sung, the Amen should always be sung by the whole assembly. Its setting should have a strong, spontaneous character. The word "Amen" should be doubled or repeated and expanded several times to give it the emphasis it deserves. There should be harmonies and instrumental embellishment, making this a most joyous conclusion to the great prayer of thanksgiving.

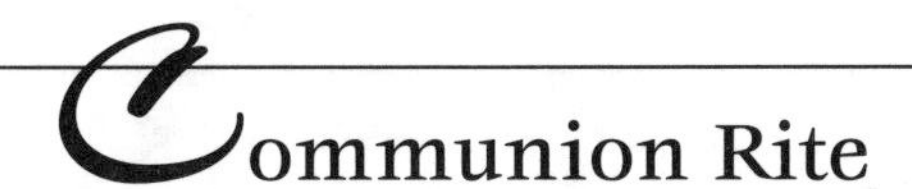

Communion Rite

Scripture

And the angel said to me, "Write this: Blessed are those who are invited to the marriage supper of the Lamb."

Revelation 19:9

Documentation

Since the eucharistic celebration is the paschal meal, it is right that the faithful . . . receive the Lord's body and blood as spiritual food. This is the purpose of the breaking of the bread and the other preparatory rites that lead directly to the communion of the people.

General Instruction of the Roman Missal, 56

The eating and drinking of the Body and Blood of the Lord in a paschal meal is the climax of our eucharistic celebration. It is prepared for by several rites: the Lord's Prayer with embolism and doxology, the rite of peace, breaking of bread (and commingling) during the "Lamb of God," private preparation of the priest, and showing of the eucharistic bread. . . . Those elements are primary which show forth signs that the first fruit of the Eucharist is the unity of the Body of Christ, Christians being loved by Christ and loving him through their love of one another. The principal texts to accompany or express the sacred action are the Lord's Prayer, the song during the communion procession, and the prayer after communion.

Music in Catholic Worship, 48

Other Sources

The communion rite . . . is a unified whole. It is a prayerful, confident, yet sober approach to the table of the Lord, acknowledging that while we are sinners, we are called to live as one in Christ, to share the Lord's table as his brothers and sisters.

Ralph Keifer

Background and Commentary

In the earliest eucharistic celebrations, the communion rite was very simple, including only the breaking of the bread and the sharing with the community. As communities of faith grew in numbers, a more elaborate structure came into being:

The Lord's Prayer
The Sign of Peace
Breaking of the Bread and Lamb of God
Invitation to Communion
Distribution of the Eucharist and Communion Song
Silent Prayer or Song of Praise
Prayer after Communion

The primary actions are the breaking of the bread, also known as the fraction rite, and the sharing of communion.

The Lord's Prayer

Scripture

Pray then in this way:
Our Father in heaven,
hallowed be your name.
Your kingdom come.
Your will be done,
on earth as it is in heaven.
Give us this day our daily bread.
And forgive us our debts,
as we also have forgiven our debtors.
And do not bring us to the time of trial,
but rescue us from the evil one.

Matthew 6:9–13

Call no one your father on earth, for you have one Father — the one in heaven.

Matthew 23:9

He said, "Abba, Father . . ."

Mark 14:36a

He was praying in a certain place, and after he had finished, one of his disciples said to him, "Lord, teach us to pray, as John taught his disciples." He said to them, "When you pray, say:
Father, hallowed be your name.
Your kingdom come.
Give us each day our daily bread.
And forgive us our sins,
for we ourselves forgive everyone indebted to us.
And do not bring us to the time of trial."

Luke 11:1–4

If you then, who are evil, know how to give good gifts to your children, how much more will the heavenly Father give the Holy Spirit to those who ask him!

Luke 11:13

We wait for the blessed hope and the manifestation of the glory of our great God and Savior, Jesus Christ.

Titus 2:13

Documentation

Lord's Prayer: this is a petition both for daily food, which for Christians means also the eucharistic bread, and for forgiveness from sin, so that what is holy may be given to those who are holy. The priest offers the invitation to pray, but all the faithful say the prayer with him; he alone adds the embolism, Deliver us, which the people conclude with a doxology. The embolism, developing the last petition of the Lord's Prayer, begs on behalf of the entire community of the faithful deliverance from the power of evil. The invitation, the prayer itself, the embolism, and the people's doxology are sung or are recited aloud.

General Instruction of the Roman Missal, **56a**

This prayer begins our immediate preparation for sharing in the Paschal Banquet. The traditional text is retained and may be set to music by composers with the same freedom as other parts of the Ordinary. All settings must provide for the participation of the priest and all present.

Music in Catholic Worship, **67**

In the eucharistic celebration there are five acclamations which ought to be sung even at Masses in which little else is sung: Alleluia; "Holy, Holy, Holy Lord"; Memorial Acclamation; Great Amen; Doxology to the Lord's Prayer.

Music in Catholic Worship, **54**

These words of praise, "For the Kingdom, the power and the glory are yours, now and forever," are fittingly sung by all, especially when the Lord's Prayer is sung. Here, too, the choir may enhance the acclamation with harmony.

Music in Catholic Worship, **59**

Other Sources

Lord, remember your Church and deliver it from all evil; make it perfect in your love and gather it from the four winds, this sanctified Church, into your kingdom which you have prepared for it, for power and glory are yours through all ages!

Didache

After . . . you say the family prayer that the Savior taught his disciples. With a pure conscience we address God as our Father and we say: "Our Father, who art in the heavens!" O how immense God's love is! . . . To those who have gone far from him and fallen into the worst evil he grants so great a pardon for their sins and makes them share so greatly in his grace that they can call him "Father."

Cyril of Jerusalem

The prayer in preparation for communion is the Our Father, in which we pray for the coming of God's kingdom. It is both the final echo of the great eucharistic prayer and the perfect prayer to accompany our sharing at the table that anticipates our sharing in the banquet of the kingdom of heaven.

Ralph Keifer

Background and Commentary

The Lord's Prayer, the most beloved and revered prayer in every tradition of Christianity, has had an important place in the eucharist since the fourth century. In the liturgy, the prayer begins with an invitation by the presider and concludes with an interpolation called the embolism, and crescendoes to the doxology "For the kingdom, the power and the glory are yours!" — a burst of praise.

The praying of the Lord's Prayer in the eucharist is communal. It is the prayer of the assembly, never the property of the choir or a soloist, not even at weddings. In my opinion, it should be spoken rather than sung; but not all music ministers share that opinion. The liturgical directives do allow for the singing of the Lord's Prayer, but in my experience this often does not work well musically. The embolism — the priest's words near the end of the prayer — can cause musical difficulties. And singing the prayer sometimes does not enhance the assembly's participation. Even in communities where this prayer is sung regularly, there are still some who will not sing the Lord's Prayer. This prayer is one of the few that are universal among Christians, and no one should ever be left out of it. When other Christians visit a Catholic celebration, this prayer makes them feel a part of the service, where many other moments may feel unfamiliar to them.

Music ministers and liturgical planners need to look at the context of the Lord's Prayer when deciding whether it should be sung. The Great Amen precedes it and the sign of peace and Lamb of God follow. When the Amen and the Lamb of God are sung, as they should be, singing the Lord's Prayer may be too much for some communities. It may also give so much emphasis to the Lord's Prayer that communion seems anticlimactic.

The posture and gesture of the assembly during this prayer has been a topic of discussion for many years. It is customary in many communities of faith that people join hands while praying the Lord's Prayer. The intention behind this is understandable and admirable, but the most appropriate posture is the *orans* position, that is, hands open and arms stretched outward. The focus of the prayer is surrender and unity for the sake of mission, not cozy intimacy. But because the gesture of holding hands arose spontaneously, often initiated by members of the assembly themselves, I would not recommend any attempt to end the practice, especially if it is an enduring, well-loved practice of the assembly. Creative catechesis may expand the assembly's understanding of the prayer beyond the intimacy of this action.

The Sign of Peace

Scripture

So when you are offering your gift at the altar, if you remember that your brother or sister has something against you, leave your gift there before the altar and go; first be reconciled to your brother or sister, and then come and offer your gift.

Matthew 5:23 – 24

Peace be to the whole community.

Ephesians 6:23a

Pursue peace with everyone, and the holiness without which no one will see the Lord.

Hebrews 12:14

Peace I leave with you; my peace I give to you.

John 14:27a

Greet one another with a kiss of love. Peace to all of you who are in Christ.

1 Peter 5:14

Documentation

Rite of peace: before they share in the same bread, the faithful implore peace and unity for the Church and for the whole human family and offer some sign of their love for one another.

General Instruction of the Roman Missal, 56b

The Conference of Bishops has left the development of specific modes of exchanging the sign of peace to local usage. Neither a specific form nor specific words are determined.

Appendix to the General Instruction, 56b

Other Sources

When we finish praying, we greet one another with a kiss.

Justin Martyr

The deacon says to all: "Greet one another with a holy kiss." The clergy then gives the kiss of peace to the bishop, laymen give it to laymen, and women to women.

Apostolic Constitutions

The deacon then says in a loud voice: "Welcome one another and embrace one another!" Do not think of this kiss as being like the kiss people exchange in the public squares when they meet friends. No, this kiss is not of that kind. It unites souls, it requires that we forget all grudges. This kiss thus signifies the union of souls with one another, and the forgetfulness of all wrongs done us. . . . This kiss, then, is an act of reconciliation.

Cyril of Jerusalem

The sign of peace was originally a full kiss on the lips, men with men, women with women. The kiss was perhaps the liturgy's most intimate gesture next to baptismal washing and anointing. . . . We today kiss everyone and on all occasions except the liturgy, where, typically, we shake hands. . . . Whatever form the sign of peace takes in a given assembly — a kiss, an embrace, or a handshake — there is no reason why the liturgical ministers must transmit it to everyone in the church. Christ's peace is abroad among the faithful assembly itself. It is not mediated to all exclusively through the liturgical minister or the clergy.

Aidan Kavanagh

Reach out and touch someone.

AT&T advertising slogan

Background and Commentary

Many see this rite as a liturgical innovation of Vatican II, but it is actually an ancient rite. It originally took place at the conclusion of the liturgy of the word, serving as an affirmation of the word and an anticipation of the eucharistic meal, echoing the biblical call to be reconciled with each other before bringing the gifts to the table. It was moved later to its current place right after the Lord's Prayer ("as we forgive those who trespass against us"). The practice began with the priest's reverencing the altar with a kiss, then passing it on to other ministers and eventually to the people who were gathered for the celebration. The gesture was a real kiss on the lips (thus the term, "kiss of peace"). This was a most intimate gesture in our worship, as Kavanagh notes, second only to the baptismal washing and anointing. As time went on, after several variations in the manner of exchanging the sign of peace, the practice disappeared. The renewal of the liturgy restored its use. The present rite begins with a short prayer and exhortation and invitation by the presiding priest. The invitation may be given by the deacon. Note that the invitation is optional, but not the sign of peace itself.

Unfortunately, this rite is often experienced as a cozy "warm fuzzy" moment between loved ones and a perfunctory acknowledgment of other people nearby. Part of this failure stems from hospitality at the beginning of the celebration that is either routine or lacking altogether. To many, it seems ludicrous and artificial to turn and greet the other people in the space after nearly an hour of ignoring them. In some communities, however, this rite is robust and lavish, and a time for genuine interaction. This usually happens where true hospitality is practiced as the community arrives for the celebration, and where community-building has been a priority over many years.

Like the Lord's Prayer, the sign of peace is a moment of unity and mission with and to one another. It is a time that calls us to be heralds of peace, not a time for surface friendliness. Some feel that the rite should be brief, but people of many ethnic communities, especially those of African, Hispanic or Polynesian heritage, find that a longer time for this rite is more satisfying. Keeping cultural differences in mind, the rite still should not become so lengthy that it overbalances other parts of the liturgy of the eucharist.

Some communities use music here, but that can give too much ritual emphasis to this moment. Music adds liturgical weight, and the Lamb of God that follows deserves the greater emphasis, since it accompanies one of the central acts of eucharist, the breaking of the bread. I find it offensive when communities sing "Let there be peace on earth" (which in my opinion is heretical: Peace does not "begin with me") or some other sentimental hymn at this moment. This is smug self-congratulation. Our focus should be on mission and service in the community and the world — to become more than we are.

Breaking of the Bread and Lamb of God

Scripture

He was oppressed, and he was afflicted, yet he did not open his mouth; like a lamb that is led to the slaughter.

Isaiah 53:7

He had been made known to them in the breaking of the bread.

Luke 24:35b

Like a sheep he was led to the slaughter, and like a lamb silent before its shearer, so he does not open his mouth. In his humiliation justice was denied him. Who can describe his generation? For his life is taken away from the earth.

Acts 8:32 – 33

The cup of blessing that we bless, is it not a sharing in the blood of Christ? The bread that we break, is it not a sharing in the body of Christ? Because there is one bread, we who are many are one body, for we all partake of the one bread.

1 Corinthians 10:16 –17

You know that you were ransomed . . . with the precious blood of Christ, like that of a lamb without defect or blemish.

1 Peter 1:18 –19

Documentation

Breaking of the bread: in apostolic times this gesture of Christ at the last supper gave the entire eucharistic action its name. This rite is not simply functional, but is a sign that in sharing in the one bread of life which is Christ we who are many are made one body (see 1 Corinthians 10:17).

***General Instruction of the Roman Missal,* 56c**

The nature of the sign demands that the material for the eucharistic celebration truly have the appearance of food.

***General Instruction of the Roman Missal,* 283**

This breaking of the bread can be done reverently during the communion rite.

***The Body of Christ,* IV, B, 2**

Agnus Dei: during the breaking of the bread and the commingling, the Agnus Dei is as a rule sung by choir or cantor with the congregation responding; otherwise it is recited aloud. This invocation may be repeated as often as necessary to accompany the breaking of the bread. The final reprise concludes with the words, grant us peace.

***General Instruction of the Roman Missal,* 56e**

The Agnus Dei is a litany-song to accompany the breaking of the bread in preparation for communion. The invocation and response may be repeated as the action demands. The final response is always "grant us peace." Unlike the "Holy, Holy, Holy Lord," and the Lord's Prayer, the "Lamb of God" is not necessarily a song of the people. Hence it may be sung by the choir, though the people should generally make the response.

Music in Catholic Worship, 68

The Lamb of God achieves greater significance at Masses when a larger sized eucharistic bread is broken for distribution and, when communion is given under both kinds, chalices must be filled. The litany is prolonged to accompany this action of breaking and pouring (GI, 56e). In this case one should not hesitate to add tropes to the litany so that the prayerfulness of the rite may be enriched.

Liturgical Music Today, 20

Litanies are often more effective when sung. The repetition of melody and rhythm draws the people together in a strong and unified response.

Music in Catholic Worship, 74

Other Sources

Just as the bread broken
was first scattered on the hills,
then was gathered and became one,
so let your Church be gathered
from the ends of the earth into your kingdom,
for yours is glory and power through the ages.

Didache

We come before you with all we have,
The work of our hands.
Broken and poured out, life for the world;
Jesus, be with us now, now.

David Haas

Whoever comes to this table
And eats of this bread
That person is saying:
I believe in a new world
A world where bread is for everyone
For the poor as much as for the rich
And everyone here who will share this cup
Shares too a covenant with the brokenhearted
And with all those who are yearning for justice.

So let us eat and drink then as he taught us —
And may this bread and this wine
Provoke a new hunger in us
That will never be satisfied
Until we taste his kingdom.

This bread that we break,
Is it not our life spread before us?
This cup that we share,
Is it not our past and tomorrow?

Tom Conry

Background and Commentary

The breaking of the bread is one of the most ancient ritual acts of the liturgy. In the early church, one large loaf of bread was broken and shared; as numbers increased, more loaves were blessed and broken. In the ninth century, the Western church mandated that the bread used for eucharist was to be unleavened. Up until that time, either leavened or unleavened bread had been used. Eastern Christians still use leavened bread. Later came the small pieces of pre-made unleavened bread, which eventually were known as hosts. When this form of bread became common, the practice of breaking of bread was obviously diminished; the symbolism of one bread broken for all was dramatically weakened. Now the church asks us to use bread that can be broken. The present directives specify that it is to be made of wheat flour and water. The bread may be made by members of the community.

The breaking of the bread, or the fraction rite, begins when the priest and other ministers begin to break the bread and pour the wine into the cups. The Lamb of God, which is to be sung, should begin immediately and continue at least until all the bread and wine is placed on the bread plates and in the cups. The music may continue in a quiet instrumental version as the priest speaks the invitation to communion.

The text of the Agnus Dei dates back to the seventh century, and was originally sung to accompany the action, as a litany that could be repeated and take some time and not be rushed. Unfortunately, we now often reduce it to a bare minimum, three invocations and responses, usually without music.

Invitation to Communion

Scripture

Happy those who feast on Wisdom
and savor her knowledge.
She will nourish and refresh them:
her bread is insight,
her drink is understanding.

Sirach 14:20, 15:3

The next day he saw Jesus coming toward him and declared, "Here is the Lamb of God who takes away the sin of the world!"

John 1:29

The next day John again was standing with two of his disciples, and as he watched Jesus walk by, he exclaimed, "Look, here is the Lamb of God!" The two disciples heard him say this, and they followed Jesus.

John 1:36

Lord, I am not worthy to have you come under my roof; but only speak the word, and my servant will be healed.

Matthew 8:8

Blessed are those who are invited to the marriage supper of the Lamb.

Revelation 19:9

Documentation

The priest then shows the eucharistic bread for communion to the faithful and with them recites the prayer of humility in words from the Gospels.

***General Instruction of the Roman Missal,* 56g**

Other Sources

Holy things to the Holy.

Eastern Rite

Background and Commentary

The invitation to communion is common to the church in both the East and in the West. It expresses strongly the role of Jesus as host, and the hospitality that Christ offers to us in sharing this meal in the most intimate relationship with him. Sharing a meal is a sacred experience, the most reverent and special of human encounters. Jesus invites us to dine with him. The invitation to communion has special significance.

If the presider sings well, it could be presented musically. Ideally, the communion song begins immediately after this invitation.

Distribution of the Eucharist and Communion Song

Scripture

I am going to rain bread from heaven for you, and each day the people shall go out and gather enough for that day.

Exodus 16:4

God spoke from above:
The skies opened,
raining down manna,
bread from the heavens.

Psalm 78:23 – 24

Drink in the richness of God,
enjoy the strength of the Lord.

Psalm 34:9

Documentation

It is most desirable that the faithful receive the Lord's body from hosts consecrated at the same Mass and that . . . they share in the chalice. Then, even through the signs, communion will stand out more clearly as a sharing in the sacrifice actually being celebrated.

General Instruction of the Roman Missal, **56h**

Holy Communion has a more complete form as a sign when it is received under both kinds. For in this manner of reception a fuller light shines on the sign of the eucharistic banquet.

General Instruction of the Roman Missal, **240**

During the . . . reception of the sacrament the communion song is sung. Its function is to express . . . union in spirit by means of the unity of their voices, [and] to give evidence of joy of heart. . . . This song begins when the priest takes communion and continues for as long as seems appropriate while the faithful receive Christ's body. The communion song should be ended in good time if there is to be a hymn after communion.

General Instruction of the Roman Missal, **56i**

The communion song should foster a sense of unity. It should be simple and not demand great effort. It gives expression to the joy of unity in the body of Christ and the fulfillment of the mystery being celebrated. Because they emphasize adoration rather than communion, most benediction hymns are not suitable. In general, during the most important seasons of the Church year, Easter, Lent, Christmas, and Advent, it is preferable that most songs used at the communion be seasonal in nature. For the remainder of the Church year, however, topical songs may be used during the communion procession, provided these texts do not conflict with the paschal character of every Sunday *(Constitution on the Sacred Liturgy,* 102, 106).

Appendix to the General Instruction, 56(i)
Music in Catholic Worship, 62

Not only does it accompany movement, and thus give order to the assembly, it also assists each communicant in the realization and achievement of "the joy of all" and the fellowship of those who "join their voices in a single song" (GI, 56i).

Liturgical Music Today, 18

Other Sources

If, therefore, you are the body of Christ and his members, your mystery has been placed on the Lord's table, you receive your mystery. You reply "Amen" to that which you are, and by replying you consent. For you hear "The body of Christ," and you reply "Amen." Be a member of the body of Christ so that your "Amen" may be true.

Augustine of Hippo

When you come forward, do not draw near with your hands wide open or with the fingers spread apart; instead, with your left hand make a throne for the right hand, which will receive. . . . Receive the body of Christ in the hollow of your hand and give the response: "Amen." . . . Then, after sharing in the body of Christ, draw near also to the cup of his blood. . . . bow in adoration and respect, and say: "Amen." Then sanctify yourself further by sharing in the blood of Christ.

Cyril of Jerusalem

I myself am the bread of life, you and I are the bread of life.

Rory Cooney

Bread for the world: a world of hunger.
Wine for all peoples: people who thirst.
May we who eat be bread for others.
May we who drink pour out our love.

Bernadette Farrell

Jesus is here right now.
Jesus is here;
With this bread and wine
his peace you'll find.
Christ Jesus is here right now.

Leon Roberts

The full sacramental sign of the eucharist, after all, is not simply eating and drinking the eucharistic supper, but rather eating and drinking together.

Ralph Keifer

To look someone in the eye, call him or her by name and place the Body of Christ in the hand is the very essence of communion.

Jan Robitscher

The communion minister who is not bread broken for the hungry and a living cup of blessing and mercy profanes the body and blood of Christ.

Ralph Keifer

I believe it is not appropriate to sing multiple communion songs . . . multiple songs tend to clutter a single liturgical action.

Michael Balhoff

If you are part of one of those rare communities that sings full-throated and lustily at communion time, God bless you.

Carole Truitt

Background and Commentary

The great liturgical scholar Gregory Dix noted that the essence of the eucharist is the fourfold action of Christ taking, blessing, breaking and giving the bread that is his body. Communion is the climax of the eucharistic action. Even though each individual takes the bread into his or her own hands, and takes the cup alone, this is a communal event. We do this together; this is the great sharing in the great feast of Christ – his salvation and redemption for the life of the world. Our communion is far more than the specific morsel of eucharistic bread that we take into our hands and consume, or the drop of a specific cup that we take in. Rather, our communion is our communion in and commitment to Christ, to Christ in each other, present in human beings, in the community. This is not a private moment with Jesus of Nazareth. This is a public time of feasting with the Risen Lord, the community, the living Body of Christ.

Song during this time is absolutely necessary but often fails. Some people say that worshipers will not sing during communion. This may be true in some places, but it is not inevitable. It is certainly possible to correct such a situation.

First, our communities have not been catechized well about the communal dimension of the real presence of Christ. Further, singing is discouraged (not always deliberately) by the music we choose, and how it is rendered. Music composed specifically for adoration of the blessed sacrament is used far too often during an action that is not adoration, but communal sharing.

Second, the song does always not "get off the ground" soon enough. If the song does not begin until after the priest and other ministers – including the ministers of music – receive communion, many of the assembly will have received communion and returned to their places by then. Not beginning the song right away reinforces the sense of communion as time for silence and meditation. Delaying the song encourages people to begin private meditation and let go of a sense of relationship with the community. At that point, why would anyone sing? Private meditation is not a bad thing, but communion is a call to relationship with the Lord made real in the sharing of the meal.

The directives call for the communion song to begin right away. Some liturgists and others suggest that the priest and other eucharistic ministers should receive communion after the rest of the assembly has received, as a sign of hospitality, thus starting the rite in a communal, assembly-centered way. This works well in some parishes. The practice, like all new practices, is a topic of discussion among liturgists and canonists; like all new practices, the question will be settled by a combination of experience and thoughtful reflection. The intent is admirable, but it seems a bit short-sighted to base it on hospitality. The priest or the eucharistic ministers are not the hosts of the gathering. There is one host of the liturgy, and that is Jesus.

No matter what the order of communion is, the song should begin right away, after the assembly responds to the invitation by saying "Lord, I am not ready to receive you." Quiet instrumental music could accompany these words, followed by the necessary announcement of the song and then, immediately, the song itself. Music ministers should receive communion after the rest of the assembly; two ministers of communion could go to the music area while the rest of the ministers are putting things away. It goes without saying that there should be enough consecrated bread and wine that everyone, including music ministers, may receive the body and blood of Christ under both species.

Third, the type of song used is important to the assembly's participation. The best congregational song is a one with a simple and easily memorized refrain; combine this with strong leadership from the cantor, and have the cantor or choir sing the verses. Look for good eucharistic texts — not sentimental personal songs about "Jesus and me," but songs that emphasize the communal nature of this moment, and focus on themes of banquet, meal, sharing and the "goodness of the Lord" (Psalm 34).

Finally, use one song only. Multiple songs with different texts, different themes and different focuses gives the impression that song at communion is mere filler, rather than an embodiment of the liturgical action of sharing together in a foretaste of the heavenly banquet. Be creative. Find songs (or adapt your present repertoire) that can be elaborated with extra verses, instrumental verses, and instrumental interludes. The song may continue after all have received, while ministers clean up and put away, but it is not necessary.

The present state of the assembly's communion song is largely due to lack of forethought by the music ministers and planners. This can be remedied with careful attention to shaping this rite and to careful attention to carrying it out over time.

Silent Prayer and Song of Praise

Scripture

Blest are you for ever, Lord,
God of our father Israel.
Power, splendor, greatness,
glory and honor are yours.

The whole universe is yours.
You are peerless in majesty,
from you flow wealth and glory.

You command all:
your hand is strength,
your hand makes strong.

And so we thank you, God.
we praise your splendid name.

1 Chronicles 29:10 – 13

With a heart full of thanks
I proclaim your wonders, God;
You are my joy, my delight;
I sing hymns to your name, Most High.

Psalm 9:2 – 3

How good to sing God praise!
How lovely the sound!

Psalm 147:1

Give thanks in all circumstances.

1 Thessalonians 5:18

Documentation

After communion, the priest and people may spend some time in silent prayer. If desired, a hymn, psalm, or other song of praise may be sung by the entire congregation.

***General Instruction of the Roman Missal,* 56j**

Silence should be observed at the designated times as part of the celebration. Its function depends on the time it occurs in each part of the celebration. . . . After communion, all praise God in silent prayer.

***General Instruction of the Roman Missal,* 23**

The singing of a psalm or hymn of praise after the distribution of communion is optional. . . . A congregational song may well provide a fitting expression of oneness in the Eucharistic Lord. Since no particular text is specified, there is ample room for creativity.

Music in Catholic Worship, 72

The proper place of silence must not be neglected, and the temptation must be resisted to cover every moment with music (GIRM, 23; GILOTH, 202; Paul VI, Apostolic Exhortation, *Evangelica Testificatio* [29 June 1971], 46). . . . Music's function is always ministerial and must never degenerate into idle background music.

Liturgical Music Today, 59

Other Sources

Halleluya!
We sing your praises, all our hearts are filled with gladness.

Christ the Lord to us said:
I am wine, I am bread,
I am wine, I am bread,
give to all who thirst and hunger.

Now he sends us all out,
strong in faith, free of doubt,
strong in faith, free of doubt,
to proclaim the joyful Gospel.

South African hymn

Let every instrument be tuned for praise!
Let all rejoice who have a voice to raise!
And may God give us faith to sing always:
Alleluia!

Fred Pratt Green

Background and Commentary

The practice of music ministers providing a meditation song after communion is problematic. The order of Mass nowhere calls for such a song. Unfortunately, it is often done to satisfy the musicians rather than the assembly. The best way to encourage meditation is to let people meditate in silence. We too often interrupt their private prayer so we can sing our favorite song. That may seem like strong language, but my intent is to raise our consciousness of what we might be communicating by our meditation song.

What the directives call for at this point in the celebration — a period of silence or a congregational song of praise — is widely ignored. This is astounding! Maybe the call for silence is ignored because we are uncomfortable with it; perhaps the song of praise is not done because of our habit of singing a meditation song, and our comfort with a closing song, which is too often experienced as exit music for the priest.

Silence provides time for the community to meditate on the mystery celebrated by the liturgy they have just enacted. This requires not a token few seconds, but an intentional, solid period of silence for prayer. Try it.

A song of praise can be a good option; and it can also solve the problem of the closing recessional song. Consider how this might work. After everyone has received communion, the presider, the ministers and the entire assembly observe a period of silent prayer. Then, either by the presider's gesture, or upon a musical introduction, the assembly stands and together all sing a rousing hymn of praise and thanksgiving. A well-known hymn, a litany of praise, or maybe even the Gloria, might be used.

Pull out all the stops — make it a joyous final act of praise and worship together! At the end of the song, the people remain standing, the presider prays the prayer after communion, leads the final blessing, proclaims the dismissal and leaves. His exit might be a procession down the center aisle with the other ministers accompanied by instrumental music; or he may exit by a side aisle and continue the ministry of hospitality and interaction with the parishioners. No congregational song is sung. The liturgy simply ends with the words of the dismissal, a call to mission.

Prayer after Communion

Scripture

You hand-fed your people
with food for angels,
heaven's bread:
ready to eat,
richly satisfying,
pleasing to every taste.

Eating this bread,
they tasted your sweetness,
the perfect meal
for their deepest hunger and hope.

Wisdom 16:20 – 21

Documentation

In the prayer after communion, the priest petitions for the effects of the mystery just celebrated and by their acclamation, Amen, the people make the prayer their own.

General Instruction of the Roman Missal, 56k

Background and Commentary

Unlike the opening prayer, this prayer after communion does not often include a specific reference to the season or feast. Neither is it a prayer of thanskgiving. This prayer is one of recall. It asks that the members of the assembly might carry the gifts of the eucharist into their lives and bring about conversion and discipleship, to live as Jesus did.

The announcements are to be made after the prayer, not before. The prayer must be connected to the eucharistic sharing; the announcements may not interrupt that connection.

Notes

chapter FOUR

The Concluding Rite

General Background

Scripture

Go therefore and make disciples of all nations, baptizing them in the name of the Father and of the Son and of the Holy Spirit, and teaching them to obey everything that I have commanded you. And remember, I am with you always, to the end of the age.

Matthew 16:19 – 20

Documentation

The concluding rite consists of: (a) the priest's greeting and blessing, which on certain days and occasions is expanded and expressed in the prayer over the people or another more solemn formulary; (b) the dismissal of the assembly, which sends each member back to doing good works, while praising and blessing the Lord.

General Instruction of the Roman Missal, 57

Background and Commentary

In any gathering of people, leave-taking and closure are important, but in the liturgy, at least, they need not be overly ritualized. The celebration of the eucharist has always had a formal conclusion, but it always has been short and to the point. In common practice, it is as follows:

Announcements
Final Blessing
Dismissal
Exit Procession of Ministers with Song

Of these elements, the final blessing requires the most careful consideration.

Announcements are a necessary part of most human gatherings. Some people who would like to do away with the announcements, but announcements are a fact of parish life. Like every other part of the Mass, they should be in proper balance with what comes before and after. The announcements should not take long. Not even major parish events, like the parish festival or a fund-raising campaign, need to be promoted with detailed announcements. Sometimes, the homily is shortened or omitted to make more time for such issues — but this should never happen. Announcements should be brief, perhaps pointing out that more details are in the parish bulletin. In most cases, someone other than the presider should lead the announcements, so that his role as leader of prayer is not compromised. All announcements to be made in the assembly should be written out in advance and reviewed with the pastor or other designated person. This will help ensure that they are to the point and appropriate.

Some parishes have the announcements in the prelude time before the liturgy formally begins, but most find that they work better here at the end of the gathering, since people will remember better what they hear at the end.

Greeting and Final Blessing

Scripture

Now the LORD said to Abram, "Go from your country and your kindred and your father's house to the land that I will show you. I will make of you a great nation, and I will bless you, and make your name great, so that you will be a blessing. I will bless those who bless you, and the one who curses you I will curse; and in you all the families of the earth shall be blessed."

Genesis 12:1–3

The LORD bless you and keep you; the LORD make his face to shine upon you, and be gracious to you; the LORD lift up his countenance upon you, and give you peace.

Numbers 6:24–26

May God bless you more and more,
Bless all your children.
May you truly be blest
by the maker of heaven and earth.

Psalm 115:14–15

Lifting up his hands, he blessed them.

Luke 24:50b

Now may the God of peace, who brought back from the dead our Lord Jesus, the great shepherd of the sheep, by the blood of the eternal covenant, make you complete in everything good so that you may do his will, working among us that which is pleasing in his sight, through Jesus Christ, to whom be the glory forever and ever. Amen.

Hebrews 13:20–21

Documentation

Then the priest, with hands outstretched, greets the people. . . . On certain days and occasions another, more solemn form of blessing or the prayer over the people precedes this form of blessing.

***General Instruction of the Roman Missal,* 124**

Background and Commentary

The final blessing is most often the familiar, simple form ("May almighty God bless you"), but there are two choices for a more developed solemn blessing. There are solemn blessings offered as options during Advent and Christmas;

on New Year's Day, Epiphany, Passion Sunday, at the Easter Vigil and on Easter Sunday; and during the season of Easter, with special formulas for Ascension and Pentecost. There are also five options for Ordinary Time. These blessings have three invocations, or tropes, to be sung or said by the presider, each followed by the assembly's Amen. The response could easily be cast in a musical form, either in the same setting as the Great Amen or with a distinct melody of its own. This works best when the presider chants or sings the tropes, but the musical response could be used even if the presider speaks them.

To give the blessing, the presider extends both hands over the assembly. A server or assisting minister may hold the book while the presider recites or sings the blessing. If this is not possible, the presider should avoid raising only one hand while holding the book. The gesture of one arm raised is too reminiscent of a Nazi salute.

The presider ends the blessing with an invocation of the Trinity while making a large sign of the cross.

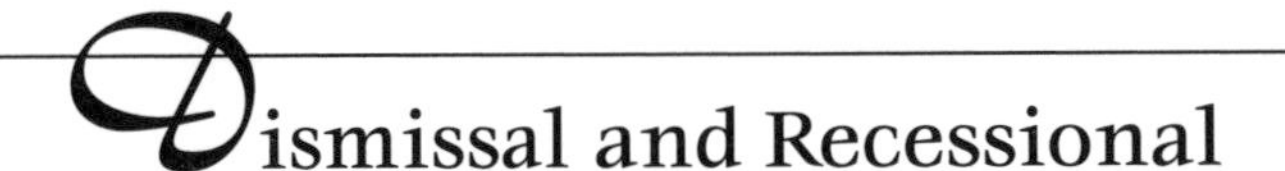

Dismissal and Recessional

Scripture

Have them make me a sanctuary, so that I may dwell among them. In accordance with all that I show you concerning the pattern of the tabernacle and of all its furniture, so you shall make it.

Exodus 25:8 – 9

If you would be happy:
never walk with the wicked,
never stand with sinners,
never sit among cynics,
but delight in the Lord's teaching
and study it night and day.

Psalm 1:1– 2

I celebrate your justice
before all the assembly;
I do not hold back the story.
Lord, you know this is true.

I did not hide in my heart
your acts of rescue;
I boldly declared to all
your truth and care, your faithful love.

Psalm 40:10 –11

All that is alive, praise. Praise the Lord.
Hallelujah!

Psalm 150:6

For you always have the poor with you, but you will not always have me.

Matthew 26:11

Daughter, your faith has made you well; go in peace, and be healed of your disease.

Mark 5:34

Documentation

The dismissal of the assembly . . . sends each member back to doing good works, while praising and blessing the Lord.

General Instruction of the Roman Missal, 57

As a rule, the priest then kisses the altar, makes the proper reverence with the ministers, and leaves.

General Instruction of the Roman Missal, 125

A recessional song is optional. The greeting, blessing, dismissal, and recessional song or instrumental music ideally form one continuous action which may culminate in the priest's personal greetings and conversations at the church door.

Music in Catholic Worship, 49

The recessional song has never been an official part of the rite; hence musicians are free to plan music which provides an appropriate closing to the liturgy. A song is one possible choice. However, if the people have sung a song after communion, it may be advisable to use only an instrumental or choir recessional.

Music in Catholic Worship, 73

Other Sources

Lord, you give the great commission:
"Heal the sick and preach the word."
Lest the Church neglect its mission,
And the Gospel go unheard,
Help us witness to your purpose
with renewed integrity;
With the Spirit's gifts empower us
for the work of ministry.

Jeffery Rowthorn

Here am I,
where underneath the bridges
in our winter cities homeless people sleep.
Here am I,
where in decaying houses little children shiver,
crying at the cold.
Where are you?

Here am I,
with people in the lineup,
anxious for a handout, aching for a job.
Here am I,
when pensioners and strikers sing and march together,
wanting something new.
Where are you?

Here am I,
where two or three are gathered,
ready to be altered, sharing wine and bread.
Here am I,
when those who hear the preaching
change their way of living,
find the way to life.
Where are you?

Brian Wren

The mission of the church is not to preserve the social order nor to conserve a specific ritual tradition. The mission of the church is to build, proclaim, and celebrate the kingdom of God.

Tom Conry

With our hands we press onward to the plow,
never turning back, we face the mystery far beyond.
With our hands, we will shape each other's stories,
we will write the vision down, never tire until it's done.

With our hands we will put our weapons down;
we will care for the earth, we will speak a word of peace.
With our hands we will wash each other's feet;
we will break the bread of justice, we will share the cup of dreams.

With our hands, we'll reach out to one another;
we will touch and heal each other, we will dry each other's tears.
With our hands we will work to build the promise,
for our God will be our strength, and like the eagle we will fly.

David Haas

Our problem is how to live what we pray, how to make our lives a daily commentary on our prayer book, how to live in consonance with what we promise, how to keep faith with the vision we pronounce.

Abraham Joshua Heschel

Send us as your blessing, Lord,
send us with the pow'r of your Spirit,
to live the Good News.
Proclaiming your gospel of peace;
that all the world will come to believe;
salvation and glory,
and wisdom and power are yours,
are yours.
Salvation and glory,
and wisdom and power are yours,
now and forevermore!

Christopher Walker

There is something incongruous about singing after the congregation has been dismissed, especially when people in most congregations are diving for purses and other paraphernalia or waiting (sometimes not so patiently) to make a quick exit without confronting or trampling Father. Instead of dragooning unwilling congregations into recessionals, we might far better provide them with a prayerful song just before the prayer after communion.

Ralph Keifer

We must regain our nerve and get on with the business of being God's people in Christ for the life of the world.

Aidan Kavanagh

Where the blind see, the lame walk, the poor have good news preached to them — there and nowhere else goes ministry.

Ralph Keifer

In liturgy as in life, the stakes are high.

Nathan Mitchell

Background and Commentary

The dismissal exhortation, the *Ite, missa est* (which means, "go, it is over"), has its origins in Roman secular events. This is a sending forth, a summary of what the entire liturgy is meant to be. In other words, the entire liturgy is a dismissal to go forth and serve, to live and act so that others may be moved to conversion by our lives and our actions as believers.

The dismissal may certainly be sung. The traditional solemn Easter dismissal is especially to be sung, if it can be done well.

The order of Mass does not prescribe or suggest a closing or recessional song. The sacramentary simply states that the ministers leave, with no mention of music. This is unnerving to many music ministers, perhaps because "we have always done it that way." They may also be concerned that the liturgy will seem unfinished without a song. But that's the point. The liturgy is not supposed to feel finished. We complete the liturgy by fulfilling the commission "to love and serve the Lord." What if those were the last words we heard and were sent forth with every Sunday?

In my experience, when there is a song of praise after communion followed by the prayer after communion, final blessing and dismissal, it can be very satisfying to omit the recessional altogether or simply do it in silence.

If there is to be a closing song, however, music ministers should find texts with strong themes of discipleship and service. The ritual choreography also needs to be considered, so that the song does not become merely traveling music for the priest and accompaniment for the gathering up of purses, coats and children.

In some communities, the members of the assembly applaud at the end of a liturgical celebration. This makes many music ministers, priests and other members of the assembly uncomfortable. If the assembly is applauding as if they were an audience clapping after a concert, that is evidence of an incorrect understanding of the role of the assembly and musicians. However, my experience is that people applaud because something good has happened, something positive, something that calls for a response. In most celebrations where applause occurs, it is a response to a spirit-filled, life-giving experience. In my opinion, liturgists can be too quick to say that applause is wrong, inappropriate or even "irreverent." Liturgy is celebration, and includes all the elements of true celebration; applause can be part of this.

Notes

Notes

Conclusion

Music in eucharistic celebration, as in any liturgical celebration, does not exist for its own sake, nor for inspiration or musical enthrallment. The purpose of music in the liturgy is to move us to conversion, to change our hearts and move us to true discipleship that centers on building the City of God. For as Amos (not usually the favorite prophet of music ministers and liturgists) reminds us:

> I hate, I despise your festivals,
> and I take no delight in your solemn assemblies.
> Even though you offer me your burnt offerings and grain offerings,
> I will not accept them;
> and the offerings of well-being of your fatted animals
> I will not look upon.
> Take away from me the noise of your songs;
> I will not listen to the melody of your harps.
> But let justice roll down like waters;
> and righteousness like an ever-flowing stream.
>
> Amos 5:21–24

Only when we surrender to the vision of what God is calling each of us to in our service as ministers of music can we truly become a living song of praise, free to celebrate the wonder of God. Then we can sing. Then we can feast at the table with our brothers and sisters honestly and in harmony with our gospel call. Then we can praise with total abandon. And then our vocation will have integrity.

> For the music of creation,
> for the song your Spirit sings,
> for your sound's divine expression,
> burst of joy in living things:
> God, our God, the world's composer,
> hear us, echoes of your voice —
> music is your art, your glory,
> let the human heart rejoice!
>
> Psalms and symphonies exalt you,
> drum and trumpet, string and reed,
> simple melodies acclaim you,
> tunes that rise from deepest need,
> hymns of longing and belonging,
> carols from a cheerful throat,
> lilt of lullaby and love song
> catching heaven in a note.

All the voices of the ages,
in transcendent chorus meet,
worship lifting up the senses,
hands that praise, and dancing feet:
over discord and division
music speaks your joy and peace,
harmony of earth and heaven,
song of God that cannot cease!

Shirley Erena Murray

Sources

Chapter One

Justin Martyr, *First Apology,* 67. Quoted in *Springtime of the Liturgy,* Lucien Deiss, ed. Collegeville: The Liturgical Press, 1979, pp. 93–94.

Paul Hallinan, archbishop of Atlanta, from a pastoral letter written in 1964. Quoted in *How Firm a Foundation: Voices of the Early Liturgical Movement,* Kathleen Hughes, RSCJ, comp. Chicago: Liturgy Training Publications (LTP), 1990, p. 121.

Virgil Michel, *The Liturgy of the Church.* New York: The Macmillan Company, 1937. Quoted in How *Firm a Foundation,* p. 187.

Eugene Walsh, "First the Assembly Gathers: The Theory," *Pastoral Music,* August/September 1982, p. 14.

Didache, 14. Quoted in *Springtime of the Liturgy,* p. 77.

The *Didascalia of the Apostles,* 13. Quoted in *Springtime of the Liturgy,* pp. 176–177.

Aidan Kavanagh, OSB, "RCIA: Not a Peanut Butter Sandwich," *Pastoral Music,* February/March 1989, p. 29.

Eugene Walsh, "Things Ain't What They Used to Be," *Pastoral Music,* August/September 1983, p. 23.

Thomas Banick, "Called and Gifted: The Assembly, the Ministers, the Musicians," *Pastoral Music,* August/September 1985, p. 13.

Karen Clarke, "The Arts as Healing Agent," *Pastoral Music,* August/September 1981, p. 29.

Eugene Walsh, "Things Ain't What They Used to Be," *Pastoral Music,* August/September 1983, p. 22.

John Gallen, SJ, "Hospitality: The Opening Rites and More," *Pastoral Music,* June/July 1986, p. 18.

Thomas Ogletree, "Hospitality to the Stranger," *Pastoral Music,* June/July 1986, p. 18.

John Gallen, SJ, "Hospitality: The Opening Rites and More," *Pastoral Music,* June/July 1986, p. 18.

Eugene Walsh, workshop

Frank Brownstead, "On Your Mark! Get Set! Sing! Ten Steps," *Pastoral Music,* June/July 1985, p. 31.

Elaine Rendler, "First, the Assembly Gathers: The Practice," *Pastoral Music,* August/September 1982, p. 16.

Bob Batastini, "Our People Just Don't Want to Sing? New Music: Step by Step," *Pastoral Music,* December/January 1978, p. 46.

James Hansen, "Congregational Singing: Like Having a Baby?" *Pastoral Music,* June/July 1985, p. 27.

Nancy Chvatal, "Don't Expect Too Much of the Psalm Poets," *Pastoral Music,* October/November 1983, p. 53.

Tom Conry, "Calling the Question: Toward a Revisionist Theology of Liturgical Music and Text," *Pastoral Music,* April/May 1981, p. 28.

William Shakespeare, *As You Like It,* act 2, scene 5.

Charles Gardner, "Ten Commandments for Liturgical Musicians," *Pastoral Music,* April/ May 1983, p. 38.

Elaine Rendler, "First, the Assembly Gathers: The Practice," *Pastoral Music,* August/September 1982, p. 17.

Bob Batastini, "Our People Just Don't Want to Sing? New Music: Step by Step," *Pastoral Music,* December/January 1978, p. 47.

Frank Brownstead, "The Catholic Liturgy and Hymns," *Pastoral Music,* June/July 1981, p. 43.

David Haas, "Song of the Body of Christ," © 1989, GIA Publications. All rights reserved.

Marty Haugen, "Gather Us In," © 1982, GIA Publications. All rights reserved.

Huub Oosterhuis, "What Is This Place?" Text and arrangement © 1967, Gooi en Sticht, bv., Baarn, The Netherlands. All rights reserved. Exclusive agent for English-language countries: OCP Publications, 5536 NE Hassalo, Portland OR 97213. All rights reserved. Used with permission.

Marty Haugen, "All Are Welcome," © 1994, GIA Publications. All rights reserved.

The *Apostolic Tradition* of Hippolytus, 42. Quoted in *Springtime of the Liturgy,* p. 153.

Romano Guardini, *Sacred Signs,* St. Louis: Pio Decimo Press, 1956. Quoted in *How Firm A Foundation,* p. 114.

Aidan Kavanagh, OSB, *Elements of Rite,* p. 77.

Roman Rite. Antiphon during the Rite of Blessing and Sprinkling Holy Water.

Easter Vigil. Acclamation during the blessing of baptismal water.

Marty Haugen, "Song over the Waters," © 1987, GIA Publications. All rights reserved.

David Haas, "Water of Life," © 1987, GIA Publications. All rights reserved.

Marty Haugen, "Song of Fire and Water," © 1984, GIA Publications. All rights reserved.

Fred Moleck, "A Tale of the Pilgrim Church," *Pastoral Music,* August/September 1983, p. 32.

Attende Domine, 10th century. Translated by Ralph Wright, OSB, © 1980, ICEL. Published as "Hear Us, Almighty Lord", #414 in *Worship,* © 1986, GIA Publications. All rights reserved.

Frederick W. Faber, "There's a Wideness in God's Mercy," public domain.

African American spiritual, "There Is a Balm in Gilead," public domain.

Rory Cooney, "Your Mercy Like Rain," © 1993, GIA Publications. All rights reserved.

David Haas, "Voices That Challenge," © 1991, GIA Publications. All rights reserved.

Rory Cooney, "As We Remember," © 1987, North American Liturgy Resources (NALR), 5536 NE Hassalo, Portland OR 97213. All rights reserved. Used with permission.

Mark Searle, *Liturgy Made Simple.* Collegeville: The Liturgical Press, 1981, pp. 36 – 37.

Eugene Walsh, workshop

Mark Searle, *Liturgy Made Simple,* p. 36.

Donna Peña, "I Say Yes," © 1989, GIA Publications. All rights reserved.

Mark Searle, *Liturgy Made Simple,* p. 36.

Chapter Two

Justin, *First Apology,* 67. Quoted in *Springtime of the Liturgy,* p. 93

Clement of Alexandria, *Paedogogus III, Hymns.* Quoted in *Springtime of the Liturgy,* p. 118

Gerard Sloyan, "Read the Bible, and . . ." *Worship* 26 (1952), p. 150 –151. Quoted in *How Firm a Foundation,* p. 226.

Ralph Keifer, "Get Thee Up on a High Mountain," *Pastoral Music,* December/January 1985, p. 47.

Anthony Krisak, "Then the Assembly Listens: The Practice," *Pastoral Music,* August/September 1982, p. 21.

Ralph Keifer, "Orthodoxy — Even in Our Music," *Pastoral Music,* April/May 1981, p. 18.

Huub Oosterhuis, "What Is This Place?" © 1967, Gooi en Sticht, bv.

Mark Searle, *Liturgy Made Simple,* p. 43.

Abraham Joshua Heschel, *Man's Quest for God.* New York: Scribner's. Copyright © renewed 1982, Hannan Susannah Heschel and Sylvia Heschel. Quoted in *A Sourcebook about Liturgy,* p. 33.

Ambrose, in *Music in Early Christian Literature,* James McKinnon, ed. New York: Cambridge University Press, 1987. Quoted in *A Sourcebook about Liturgy,* pp. 32 – 33.

Mark Searle, *Liturgy Made Simple,* pp. 44 – 45.

Brian Wren, "Stand Up, Friends!" © 1986, Hope Publishing Co., Carol Stream IL 60188. All rights reserved. Used by permission.

Miriam Therese Winter, "What's Wrong with *Music in Catholic Worship,*" *Pastoral Music,* February/March 1985, p. 16.

Justin, *First Apology,* 67. Quoted in *Springtime of the Liturgy,* p. 93.

Bishop Kenneth Untener, "Musicians and Clergy: Emerging Ministers," *Pastoral Music,* August/September 1983, p. 40.

Aidan Kavanagh, OSB, *Elements of Rite.* Collegeville: The Liturgical Press, 1982, p. 26.

Roman Rite. Assent to the profession of faith.

David Haas, "Blest Are They," © 1985, GIA Publications. All rights reserved.

Henry Alford, "We Walk by Faith," public domain.

Ignatius of Antioch, *Ad Trallenses,* 9. Quoted in *Springtime of the Liturgy,* p. 38.

Zimbabwean traditional, published as "If You Believe and I Believe," #825 in *RitualSong,* GIA.

Patrick Collins, "Establish the Importance of What Is Important: The Word," *Pastoral Music,* April/May 1977, p. 26.

Tad Guzie, "The Art of Assembling," *Pastoral Music,* April/May 1987, p. 24.

Chapter Three

Huub Oosterhuis, "What Is This Place?" © 1967, Gooi en Sticht, bv.

Bishops' Committee on the Liturgy *Newsletter,* 8:7– 8, July – August 1972.

Michael Balhoff, Gary Daigle, Darryl Ducote, "Table Prayer," © 1985 by Domean Music. Used by permission of GIA Publications, Inc., exclusive agent. All rights reserved.

Michael Joncas, "We Come to Your Feast," © 1994, GIA Publications. All rights reserved.

Jaroslav J. Vajda, "Now the Silence," © 1969, Hope Publishing Co., Carol Stream IL 60188. All rights reserved. Used by permission.

Justin, *First Apology,* 65. Quoted in *Springtime of the Liturgy,* p. 92.

The *Kiddush,* Jewish blessing for Sabbath and feast days. Quoted in *Springtime of the Liturgy,* p. 5 – 6.

Birkat ha-mazon, Jewish blessing after meals. Quoted in *Springtime of the Liturgy,* pp. 7– 8.

Thomas Porter, "The Eucharistic Prayer's Basic Elements: Praise, Thanksgiving, Intercession," *Pastoral Music,* December/January 1986, p. 28.

Edward Foley, "Let Us Pray: 'In God We Trust . . .' " *Pastoral Music,* October/November 1985, p. 28.

Ralph Keifer, "The Eucharistic Prayer, Part II: Restoring the Assembly's Role," *Pastoral Music,* December/January 1982, p. 15.

Mary McGann, "Find the Meaning of the Eucharistic Prayer in Its Sung Form," *Pastoral Music,* June/July 1983, p. 48.

Peter Fink, SJ, "Music and the Eucharistic Prayer," *Pastoral Music,* February/ March 1982, p. 48.

Robert Haas, "Music Education in the Parish: A Dream," in *Children, Liturgy and Music: Pastoral Music in Practice,* Washington: Pastoral Press, 1980, p. 118.

The *Apostolic Tradition* of Hippolytus. Quoted in *Springtime of the Liturgy,* p. 129 –130.

Clement of Rome, Letter to the Corinthians, 34, 5 – 8. Quoted in *Springtime of the Liturgy,* pp. 81– 82.

The *Catecheses* of Cyril of Jerusalem 23, 6. Quoted in *Springtime of the Liturgy,* p. 285.

Peter Fink, SJ, "Music and the Eucharistic Prayer," *Pastoral Music,* February/March 1982, p. 49.

The *Catecheses* of Cyril of Jerusalem 23, 7. Quoted in *Springtime of the Liturgy,* p. 285.

The *Euchology* of Der Balyzeh, anaphora. Quoted in *Springtime of the Liturgy,* pp. 247– 248.

Peter Fink, SJ, "Music and the Eucharistic Prayer," *Pastoral Music,* February/March 1982, p. 49.

Marty Haugen, "We Remember," © 1980, GIA Publications. All rights reserved.

The *Euchology* of Der Balyzeh, liturgy of the Mass. Quoted in *Springtime of the Liturgy,* pp. 245 – 246.

Marty Haugen, "Eucharistic Prayer II," © 1990, GIA Publications. All rights reserved.

Justin, *First Apology,* 65. Quoted in *Springtime of the Liturgy,* p. 92.

Mark Searle, *Liturgy and Social Justice,* Collegeville: The Liturgical Press, 1980. Quoted in *A Sourcebook about Liturgy,* p. 84.

Peter Fink, SJ, "Music and the Eucharistic Prayer," *Pastoral Music,* February/March 1982, p. 49.

Barbara Schmich, "Amen" in *Assembly* (Notre Dame Center for Pastoral Liturgy), February 1981. Quoted in *A Sourcebook about Liturgy,* p. 59.

Ralph Keifer, "When We Eat This Bread and Drink This Cup . . ." *Pastoral Music,* April/May 1991, p. 25.

The *Didache,* 9 –10. Quoted in *Springtime of the Liturgy,* p. 76.

The *Catecheses* of Cyril of Jerusalem 23, 11. Quoted in *Springtime of the Liturgy,* p. 286.

Ralph Keifer, "When We Eat This Bread and Drink This Cup . . ." *Pastoral Music,* April/May 1991, p. 25.

Justin, *First Apology,* 65. Quoted in *Springtime of the Liturgy,* p. 92.

The *Apostolic Constitutions* of Hippolytus, VIII, 11, 7– 9. Quoted in *Springtime of the Liturgy,* p. 227.

The *Catecheses* of Cyril of Jerusalem, 23, 3. Quoted in *Springtime of the Liturgy,* p. 284.

Aidan Kavanagh, OSB, *Elements of Rite,* p. 66.

AT&T advertising slogan.

The *Didache,* 9 –10. Quoted in *Springtime of the Liturgy,* p. 75.

David Haas, "Jesus, Be with Us Now," © 1997, GIA Publications. All rights reserved.

Tom Conry, "This Bread," © 1981, New Dawn Music, 5536 NE Hassalo, Portland OR 97213. All rights reserved. Used with permission.

Augustine, in Daniel J. Sheerin, *Message of the Fathers of the Church: The Eucharist.* Wilmington DE: Michael Glazier, 1986. Quoted in *A Sourcebook about Liturgy,* p. 90.

The *Catecheses* of Cyril of Jerusalem, 23, 22. Quoted in *Springtime of the Liturgy,* p. 289.

Rory Cooney, "Bread of Life," © 1987, North American Liturgy Resources (NALR), 5536 NE Hassalo, Portland OR 97213. All rights reserved. Used with permission.

Bernadette Farrell, "Bread for the World," © 1991, Bernadette Farrell. Published by OCP Publications, Inc., 5536 NE Hassalo, Portland OR 97213. All rights reserved. Used by permission.

Leon Roberts, "Jesus Is Here," © 1986, GIA Publications. All rights reserved.

Ralph Keifer, "When We Eat This Bread and Drink This Cup . . ." *Pastoral Music,* April/May 1991, p. 28.

Jan Robitscher, "Elements of Rite for the (dis)Abled," *Pastoral Music,* February/March 1985, p. 36.

Ralph Keifer, "When We Eat This Bread and Drink This Cup . . ." *Pastoral Music,* April/May 1991, p. 28.

Michael Balhoff, "What Did You Do Good Last Sunday?" *Pastoral Music,* December/January 1978, p. 18.

Carole Truitt, "Should We Sing During Communion? Yes and No," *Pastoral Music,* April/May 1991, p. 46.

South African text and tune, © 1984 Utrick, Walton Music Corporation, agent. Published as #692 in *Ritualsong,* © 1996, GIA.

Fred Pratt Green, "When in Our Music God Is Glorified," © 1972, Hope Publishing Co., Carol Stream IL 60188. All rights reserved. Used by permission.

Chapter Four

Jeffery Rowthorn, "Lord, You Give the Great Commission," © 1978, Hope Publishing Co., Carol Stream IL 60188. All rights reserved. Used by permission.

Brian Wren, "Here Am I," © 1983, Hope Publishing Co., Carol Stream IL 60188. All rights reserved. Used by permission.

David Haas, "E Na Lima Hana (The Working Hands)," © 1997, GIA Publications. All rights reserved.

Christopher Walker, "Send Us as Your Blessing, Lord," © 1987, Christopher Walker. Published by OCP Publications, 5536 NE Hassalo, Portland OR 97213. All rights reserved. Used with permission.

Ralph Keifer, "When We Eat This Bread and Drink This Cup . . ." *Pastoral Music,* April/May 1991, p. 27.

Aidan Kavanagh, OSB, "RCIA: Not a Peanut Butter Sandwich," *Pastoral Music,* February/March 1989, p. 30.

Tom Conry, "Calling the Question: Toward a Revisionist Theology of Music and Text," *Pastoral Music,* April/May 1981, p. 26.

Abraham Joshua Heschel, *Man's Quest for God.* Quoted in *A Sourcebook about Liturgy,* p. 103.

Ralph Keifer, "A View from the Pew," *Pastoral Music,* October/November 1985, p. 40.

Nathan Mitchell, "The Amen Corner," *Worship,* September 1992. Quoted in *A Sourcebook of Liturgy,* p. 161.

Conclusion

Shirley Erena Murray, "For the Music of Creation," © 1992, Hope Publishing Co., Carol Stream IL 60188. All rights reserved. Used by permission.